Profiting From The Word

PROFITING FROM THE WORD

Arthur Pinkington

A. W. PINK   1886– 1952

72-575470

208

c†

THE BANNER OF TRUTH TRUST

THE BANNER OF TRUTH TRUST
3 Murrayfield Road, Edinburgh EH12 6EL
P.O. Box 652, Carlisle, Pennsylvania 17013, USA
First published in this form 1970
Reprinted 1974
ISBN 0 85151 032 9

Set in 11 point Imprint and printed in Great Britain by
Hazell Watson & Viney Ltd, Aylesbury, Bucks

Contents

Publishers' Preface

THE written ministry of A. W. Pink was one of the least noticed facts of major significance in the first half of the twentieth century. In 1921 he commenced a monthly magazine, *Studies in the Scriptures*, which was maintained almost entirely by his own pen for over thirty years. Through that period the number of his readers probably never rose much above a thousand. This did not deter Arthur Pink. He believed he knew the deficiencies which had led to the prevailing spiritual weakness and he gave himself unreservedly to ministering to the hundreds across the world who read his magazine from cover to cover. The aim was to give Christians such biblical expositions as would produce clear heads and holy lives and prayer and godliness, and if the circle of readers was small it was distinguished by a common, serious commitment to historic Christianity.

It is since Pink's death in 1952, and more particularly since the awakening of a wider interest in the truths which he maintained so faithfully, that his writings have become more generally known and valued. A number of the expository and doctrinal series originally included in his magazine have recently been reprinted on both sides of the Atlantic.

The series which forms this new book was also first published in *Studies in the Scriptures*. They reveal the devotion to Scripture and the searching experimental note which are characteristic of Pink at his best. The Trust is glad to be able to place this volume alongside those already published, *The Sovereignty of God* and *The Life of Elijah*.

1: *The Scriptures and Sin*

THERE is grave reason to believe that much Bible reading and Bible study of the last few years has been of no spiritual profit to those who engaged in it. Yea, we go further; we greatly fear that in many instances it has proved a curse rather than a blessing. This is strong language, we are well aware, yet no stronger than the case calls for. Divine gifts may be misused, and Divine mercies abused. That this has been so in the present instance is evident by the fruits produced. Even the natural man may (and often does) take up the study of the Scriptures with the same enthusiasm and pleasure as he might of the sciences. Where this is the case, his store of knowledge is increased, and so also is his pride. Like a chemist engaged in making interesting experiments, the intellectual searcher of the Word is quite elated when he makes some discovery in it; but the joy of the latter is no more spiritual than would be that of the former. Again, just as the successes of the chemist generally increase his sense of self-importance and cause him to look with disdain upon others more ignorant than himself, so alas, is it often the case with those who have investigated Bible numerics, typology, prophecy and other such subjects.

The Word of God may be taken up from various motives. Some read it to satisfy their literary pride. In certain circles it has become both the respectable and popular thing to obtain a general acquaintance with the contents of the Bible simply because it is regarded as an educational defect to be ignorant of them. Some read it to satisfy their sense of curiosity, as they might any other book of note. Others read it to satisfy their sectarian pride. They consider it a duty to be well versed in the particular tenets of their own denomination and so search eagerly for proof-texts in support of '*our* doctrines.' Yet others read it for the purpose of being able to argue successfully with those who differ from them. But in all this there is no thought of God, no yearning for spiritual edification, and therefore no real benefit to the soul.

Of what, then, does a true profiting from the Word consist? Does not 2 Timothy 3:16, 17 furnish a clear answer to our question? There we read, 'All scripture is given by inspiration of God, and is profitable for doctrine, for reproof, for correction, for instruction in righteousness: that the man of God may be perfect, throughly furnished unto all good works.' Observe what is here omitted: the Holy Scriptures are given us not for intellectual gratification and carnal speculation, but to furnish unto 'all good works,' and that by teaching, reproving, correcting us. Let us endeavour to amplify this by the help of other passages.

1. An individual is spiritually profited when the Word *convicts him of sin*. This is its first office: to reveal our depravity, to expose our vileness, to make known our wickedness. A man's moral life may be irreproachable, his dealings with his fellows faultless; but when the Holy Spirit applies the Word to his heart and conscience, opening his sin-blinded eyes to see his relation and attitude to God, he cries, 'Woe is me, for I am undone.' It is in this way that each truly saved soul is brought to realize his need of Christ. 'They that are whole need not a physician, but

they that are sick' (Luke 5:31). Yet it is not until the Spirit applies the Word in Divine power that any individual is made to feel that he *is* sick, sick unto death.

Such conviction that brings home to the heart the awful ravages which sin has wrought in the human constitution is not to be restricted to the initial experience which immediately precedes conversion. Each time that God blesses His Word to my heart, I am made to feel how far, far short I come of the standard which He has set before me, namely, 'Be ye holy in *all* manner of conversation' (I Peter 1:15). Here, then, is the first test to apply: as I read of the sad failures of different ones in Scripture, does it make me realize how sadly like unto them I am? As I read of the blessed and perfect life of Christ, does it make me recognize how terribly unlike Him I am?

2. An individual is spiritually profited when the Word makes him *sorrow over sin*. Of the stony-ground hearer it is said that he 'heareth the word, and anon with joy receiveth it; yet hath he not root in himself' (Matt. 13:20, 21); but of those who were convicted under the preaching of Peter it is recorded that they were pricked in their heart' (Acts 2:37). The same contrast exists today. Many will listen to a flowery sermon, or an address on 'dispensational truth' that displays oratorical powers or exhibits the intellectual skill of the speaker, but which, usually, contains no searching application to the conscience. It is received with approbation, but no one is humbled before God or brought into a closer walk with Him through it. But let a faithful servant of the Lord (who by grace is not seeking to acquire a reputation for his 'brilliance') bring the teaching of Scripture to bear upon character and conduct, exposing the sad failures of even the best of God's people, and, though the crowd will despise the messenger, the truly regenerate will

be thankful for the message which causes them to mourn before God and cry, 'Oh, wretched man that I am.' So it is in the private reading of the Word. It is when the Holy Spirit applies it in such a way that I am made to see and feel my inward corruptions that I am really blessed.

What a word is that in Jeremiah 31:19: 'After that I was instructed, I smote upon my thigh: I was ashamed, yea, even confounded.'! Do you, my reader, know anything of such an experience? Does your study of the Word produce a broken heart and lead to a humbling of yourself before God? Does it convict you of your sins in such a way that you are brought to daily repentance before Him? The paschal lamb had to be eaten with 'bitter herbs' (Ex. 12:8); so as we really feed on the Word, the Holy Spirit makes it 'bitter' to us before it becomes sweet to our taste. Note the order in Revelation 10:9, 'And I went unto the angel, and said unto him, Give me the little book. And he said unto me, Take it, and eat it up; and it shall make thy belly bitter, but it shall be in thy mouth sweet as honey.' This is ever the experimental order: there must be mourning before comfort (Matt. 5:4); humbling before exalting (I Pet. 5:6).

3. An individual is spiritually profited when the Word leads to *confession of sin*. The Scriptures are profitable for 'reproof' (2 Tim. 3:16), and an honest soul will acknowledge its faults. Of the carnal it is said, 'For every one that loveth evil hateth the light, neither cometh to the light, lest his deeds should be reproved' (John 3:20). 'God be merciful to me a sinner' is the cry of a renewed heart, and every time we are quickened by the Word (Psa. 119) there is a fresh revealing to us and a fresh owning by us of our transgressions before God. 'He that covereth his sins shall not prosper: but whoso confesseth and forsaketh them shall

have mercy' (Prov. 28:13). There can be no spiritual prosperity or fruitfulness (Psa. 1:3) while we conceal within our breasts our guilty secrets; only as they are freely owned before God, and that in detail, shall we enjoy His mercy.

There is no real peace for the conscience and no rest for the heart while we bury the burden of unconfessed sin. Relief comes when it is fully unbosomed to God. Mark well the experience of David, 'When I kept silence, my bones waxed old through my roaring all the day long. For day and night thy hand was heavy upon me: my moisture is turned into the drought of summer' (Psa. 32:3, 4). Is this figurative but forcible language unintelligible unto you? Or does your own spiritual history explain it? There is many a verse of Scripture which no commentary save that of personal experience can satisfactorily interpret. Blessed indeed is the immediate sequel here: 'I acknowledged my sin unto thee, and mine iniquity have I not hid. I said, I will confess my transgressions unto the Lord; and thou forgavest the iniquity of my sin' (Psa. 32:5).

4. An individual is spiritually profited when the Word produces in him *a deeper hatred of sin*. 'Ye that love the Lord, hate evil' (Psa. 97:10). 'We cannot love God without hating that which He hates. We are not only to avoid evil, and refuse to continue in it, but we must be up in arms against it, and bear towards it a hearty indignation' (C. H. Spurgeon). One of the surest tests to apply to the professed conversion is the heart's attitude towards sin. Where the principle of holiness has been planted, there will necessarily be a loathing of all that is unholy. If our hatred of evil be genuine, we are thankful when the Word reproves even the evil which we suspected not.

This was the experience of David: 'Through thy precepts I get understanding: therefore I hate every false way' (Psa. 119:104). Observe well, it is not merely 'I abstain from,' but 'I hate'; not only 'some' or 'many,' but '*every* false way'; and not only 'every evil,' but 'every *false* way.' 'Therefore I esteem all thy precepts concerning all things to be right, and I hate every false way' (Psa. 119: 128). But it is the very opposite with the wicked: 'Seeing thou hatest instruction, and castest my words behind thee' (Psa. 50:17). In Proverbs 8:13, we read, 'The fear of the Lord is to hate evil,' and this godly fear comes through reading the Word: see Deuteronomy 17:18, 19. Rightly has it been said, 'Till sin be hated, it cannot be mortified; you will never cry against it, as the Jews did against Christ, Crucify it, Crucify it, till sin be really abhorred as He was' (Edward Reyner, 1635).

5. An individual is spiritually profited when the Word causes *a forsaking of sin.* 'Let every one that nameth the name of Christ depart from iniquity' (2 Tim. 2:19). The more the Word is read with the definite object of discovering what is pleasing and what is displeasing to the Lord, the more will His will become known; and if our hearts are right with Him the more will our ways be conformed thereto. There will be a 'walking in the truth' (3 John 4). At the close of 2 Corinthians 6 some precious promises are given to those who separate themselves from unbelievers. Observe, there, the application which the Holy Spirit makes of them. He does not say, 'Having therefore these promises, be comforted and become complacent thereby,' but 'Having therefore these promises, dearly beloved, let us *cleanse ourselves* from all filthiness of the flesh and spirit' (2 Cor. 7:1).

'Now ye are *clean* through the word which I have spoken unto you' (John 15:3). Here is another important rule by which we should frequently test ourselves: Is the reading and studying of God's Word producing a *purging* of my ways? Of old the question was asked, 'Wherewithal shall a young man cleanse his way?' and the Divine answer is 'by taking heed thereto according to thy word.' Yes, not simply by reading, believing, or memorizing it, but by the personal application of the Word to our 'way.' It is by 'taking heed' to such exhortations as '*Flee* fornication' (I Cor. 6:18), '*Flee* from idolatry' (1 Cor. 10:14). '*Flee* these things' – a covetous love for money (1 Tim. 6:11), '*Flee* also youthful lusts' (2 Tim. 2:22), that the Christian is brought into practical separation from evil; for sin has not only to be confessed but 'forsaken' (Prov. 28:13).

6. An individual is spiritually profited when the Word *fortifies against sin*. The Holy Scriptures are given to us not only for the purpose of revealing our innate sinfulness, and the many, many ways in which we 'come short of the glory of God' (Rom 3:23), but also to teach us how to obtain deliverance from sin, how to be kept from displeasing God. 'Thy word have I hid in mine heart, that I *might not sin* against thee' (Psa. 119:11). This is what each of us is required to do: 'Receive, I pray thee, the law from his mouth, and lay up his words in thine heart' (Job 22:22). It is particularly the commandments, the warnings, the exhortations, we need to make our own and to treasure; to memorize them, meditate upon them, pray over them, and put them into practice. The only effective way of keeping a plot of ground from being overgrown by weeds is to sow good seed therein: 'Overcome evil with good' (Rom 12:21). So the more Christ's Word dwells in us 'richly' (Col. 3:16), the less room will there be for the exercise of sin in our hearts and lives.

It is not sufficient merely to assent to the veracity of the Scriptures, they require to be received into the affections.

It is unspeakably solemn to note that the Holy Spirit specifies as the ground of apostasy, 'because the *love of* the truth they *received not*' (2 Thess. 2:10, Greek). 'If it lie only in the tongue or in the mind, only to make it a matter of talk and speculation, it will soon be gone. The seed which lies on the surface, the fowls in the air will pick up. Therefore hide it deeply; let it get from the ear into the mind, from the mind into the heart; let it soak in further and further. It is only when it hath a prevailing sovereignty in the heart that we receive it in the love of it – when it is dearer than our dearest lust, then it will stick to us' (Thomas Manton).

Nothing else will preserve from the infections of this world, deliver from the temptations of Satan, and be so effective a preservative against sin, as the Word of God received into the affections, 'The law of his God is in his heart; none of his steps shall slide' (Psa. 37:31). As long as the truth is active within us, stirring the conscience, and is really loved by us, we shall be kept from falling.   When Joseph was tempted by Potiphar's wife, he said, 'How then can I do this great wickedness, and sin against God?' (Gen. 39:9). The Word was in his heart, and therefore had prevailing power over his lusts. The ineffable holiness, the mighty power of God, who is able both to save and to destroy. None of us knows when he may be tempted: therefore it is necessary to be prepared against it. 'Who among you will give ear . . . and hear *for the time to come*?' (Isa. 42:23). Yes, we are to anticipate the future and be fortified against it, by storing up the Word in our hearts for coming emergencies.

7. An individual is spiritually profited when the Word causes him to *pratice the opposite of sin*. 'Sin is the transgression of the law' (1 John 3:4). God says 'Thou shalt,'

sin says 'I will not'; God says 'Thou shalt not,' sin says 'I will.' Thus, sin is rebellion against God, the determination to have my own way (Isa. 53:6). Therefore sin is a species of anarchy in the spiritual realm, and may be likened unto the waving of the red flag in the face of God. Now the opposite of sinning against God is submission to Him, as the opposite of lawlessness is subjection to the law. Thus, to practise the opposition of sin is to walk in the path of obedience. This is another chief reason why the Scriptures were given: to *make known* the path which is pleasing to God for us. They are profitable not only for reproof and correction, but also for 'instruction in righteousness.'

Here, then, is another important rule by which we should frequently test ourselves. Are my thoughts being formed, my heart controlled, and my ways and works regulated by God's Word? This is what the Lord requires: 'Be ye *doers of* the word, and not hearers only, deceiving your own selves' (James 1:22). This is how gratitude to and affection for Christ are to be expressed: 'If ye love me, *keep* my commandments' (John 14:15). For this, Divine assistance is needed. David prayed, 'Make me to go in the path of thy commandments' (Psa. 119:35). 'We need not only light to know our way, but a heart to walk in it. Direction is necessary because of the blindness of our minds; and the effectual impulsions of grace are necessary because of the weakness of our hearts. It will not answer our duty to have a naked notion of truths, unless we embrace and pursue them' (Manton). Note it is 'the *path* of thy commandments': not a self-chosen course, but a definitely marked one; not a public 'road,' but a private 'path.'

Let both writer and reader honestly and diligently measure himself, as in the presence of God, by the seven things here enumerated. Has your study of the Bible made

you more humble, or more proud – proud of the knowledge you have acquired? Has it raised you in the esteem of
your fellow men, or has it led you to take a lower place before God? Has it produced in you a deeper abhorrence and
loathing of self, or has it made you more complacent? Has
it caused those you mingle with, or perhaps teach, to *say*, I
wish I had your *knowledge* of the Bible; or does it cause
you to *pray*, Lord give me the faith, the grace, the *holiness*
Thou hast granted my friend, or teacher? 'Meditate upon
these things; give thyself wholly to them; that thy profiting *may appear* unto all' (1 Tim. 6:15).

2: *The Scriptures and God*

THE Holy Scriptures are wholly super-natural. They are a Divine revelation. 'All scripture is given by inspiration of God' (2 Tim. 3:16). It is not merely that God elevated men's minds, but that He directed their thoughts. It is not simply that He communicated concepts to them, but that He dictated the very words they used. 'The prophecy came not in old time by the will of man: but holy men of God spake as they were moved by the Holy Spirit' (2 Peter 1:21). Any human 'theory' which denies their *verbal* inspiration is a device of Satan's, an attack upon God's truth. The Divine image is stamped upon every page. Writings so holy, so heavenly, so awe-producing, could not have been created by man.

The Scriptures make known a *supernatural* God. That may be a very trite remark, yet today it needs making. The 'god' which is believed in by many professing Christians is becoming more and more paganized. The prominent place which 'sport' now has in the nation's life, the excessive love of pleasure, the abolition of home-life, the brazen immodesty of women, are so many symptoms of the same disease which brought about the downfall and death of the empires of Babylon, Persia, Greece and Rome. And the twentieth-century idea of God which is entertained by the majority of people in lands nominally 'Christian' is rapidly approximating to the character ascribed to the gods of the ancients. In sharp contrast therewith, the God of Holy Writ is clothed with such perfections and vested with such attributes that no mere human intellect could possibly have invented them.

God can only be known by means of a *supernatural revelation* of Himself. Apart from the Scriptures, even a theoretical acquaintance with Him is impossible. It still holds true that 'the world by wisdom knew not God' (1 Cor. 1:21). Where the Scriptures are ignored, God is 'the unknown God' (Acts 17:23). But something more than the Scriptures is required before the soul can *know* God, know him in a real, personal, vital way. This seems to be recognized by few today. The prevailing practice assumes that a knowledge of God can be obtained through studying the Word, in the same way as a knowledge of chemistry may be secured by mastering its textbooks. An intellectual knowledge of God maybe; not so a spiritual one. A supernatural God can only be known supernaturally (i.e. known in a manner *above* that which mere nature can acquire), by a supernatural revelation of Himself to the heart. 'God, who commanded the light to shine out of darkness, hath shined in our hearts, to give the light of the knowledge of the glory of God in the face of Jesus Christ' (2 Cor. 4:6). The one who has been favoured with this supernatural experience has learned that only 'in thy light shall we see light' (Psa. 36:9).

God can only be known through a *supernatural faculty*. Christ made this clear when He said, 'Except a man be born again, he cannot see the kingdom of God' (John 3:3). The unregenerate have no spiritual knowledge of God. 'The natural man receiveth not the things of the Spirit of God: for they are foolishness unto him: neither can he know them, because they are *spiritually* discerned' (1 Cor. 2:14). Water, of itself, never rises above its own level. So the natural man is incapable of perceiving that which transcends mere nature. 'This is life eternal, that they might know thee the only true God' (John 17:3). Eternal life must be imparted before the 'true God' can be known. Plainly is this affirmed in 1 John 5:20, 'We know that the Son of God is come, and hath given us an understanding, that we may know Him that is true.' Yes, an 'understanding,' a spiritual understanding, by new creation, must be given *before* God can be known in a spiritual way.

A supernatural knowledge of God produces *a supernatural experience*, and this is something to which multitudes of church members are total strangers. Most of the 'religion' of the day is but a touching up of 'old Adam.' It is merely a garnishing of sepulchres full of corruption. It is an outward 'form.' Even where there is a sound creed, only too often it is a dead orthodoxy. Nor should this be wondered at. It has ever been thus. It was so when Christ was here upon earth. The Jews were very orthodox. At that time they were free from idolatry. The temple stood at Jerusalem, the Law was expounded, Jehovah was worshipped. And yet Christ said to them, 'He that sent me is true, whom ye know not.' (John 7:28). 'Ye neither know me, nor my Father: if ye had known me, ye should have known my Father also' (John 8:19). 'It is my Father that honoureth me; of whom ye say, that he is your God. Yet ye have not known him' (John 8:54, 55). And mark it well, this is said to a people who had the Scriptures, searched them diligently, and venerated them as God's Word! They were well acquainted with God theoretically, but a spiritual knowledge of Him they had not.

As it was in the Jewish world, so it is in Christendom.

21

Multitudes who 'believe' in the Holy Trinity are completely devoid of a supernatural or spiritual knowledge of God. How are we so sure of this? In this way: the character of the fruit reveals the character of the tree that bears it; the nature of the waters makes known the nature of the fountain from which they flow. A supernatural knowledge of God produces a supernatural experience, and a supernatural experience results in *supernatural fruit*. That is to say, God actually dwelling in the heart revolutionizes, transforms the life. There is that brought forth which mere nature cannot produce, yea, that which is directly contrary thereto. And this is noticeably absent from the lives of perhaps ninety-five out of every hundred now professing to be God's children. There is nothing in the life of the average professing Christian except what can be accounted for on natural grounds. But in the genuine child of God it is far otherwise. He is, in truth, a miracle of grace; he is a 'new creature in Christ Jesus' (2 Cor. 5:17). His experience, his life, is supernatural.

The supernatural experience of the Christian is seen in his *attitude toward God*. Having within him the life of God, having been made a 'partaker of the Divine nature' (2 Pet. 1:4), he necessarily loves God, loves the things of God, loves what God loves; and, contrariwise, he hates what God hates. This supernatural experience is wrought in him by the Spirit of God, and that by means of the Word of God. The Spirit never works apart from the Word. By that Word He quickens. By that Word He produces conviction of sin. By that Word He sanctifies. By that Word He gives assurance. By that Word He makes the saint to grow. Thus each one of us may ascertain the extent to which we are profiting from our reading and studying of the Scriptures by the *effects* which they are, through the

Spirit's application of them, *producing in us*. Let us enter now into details. He who is truly and spiritually profiting from the Scriptures has:

1. *A clearer recognition of God's claims*. The great controversy between the Creator and the creature has been whether He or they should be God, whether His wisdom or theirs should be the guiding principle of their actions, whether His will or theirs should be supreme. That which brought about the fall of Lucifer was his resentment at being in subjection to his Maker: 'Thou hast said in thine heart, I will ascend into heaven, I will exalt my throne above the stars of God . . . I will be like the most High' (Isa. 14:13, 14). The lie of the serpent which lured our first parents to their destruction was, 'Ye shall be as gods' (Gen. 3:5). And ever since then the heart-sentiment of the natural man has been, 'Depart from us; for we desire not the knowledge of thy ways. What is the Almighty, that we should serve him?' (Job 21:14, 15). 'Our lips are our own; who is Lord over us?' (Psa. 12:4). 'We are lords; we will come no more unto thee' (Jer. 2:31).

Sin has alienated man from God (Eph. 4:18). His heart is averse to Him, his will is opposed to His, his mind is at enmity against Him. Contrariwise, *salvation* means being restored to God: 'For Christ also hath once suffered for sins, the just for the unjust, that he might *bring us to God*' (1 Pet. 3:18). Legally that has already been done; experimentally it is in the process of accomplishment. Salvation means being reconciled to God; and that involves and includes sin's dominion over us being broken, enmity within us being slain, the heart being won to God. This is what true conversion is; it is a tearing down of every idol, a renouncing of the empty vanities of a cheating world, and taking God for our portion, our ruler, our all in all. Of the

Corinthians we read that they 'first gave their own selves unto the Lord' (2 Cor. 8:5). The desire and determination of those truly converted is that they 'should not henceforth live unto themselves, but unto him which died for them, and rose again' (2 Cor. 5:15).

God's claims are now recognized, His rightful dominion over us is acknowledged, He is owned *as* God. The converted yield themselves 'unto God, as those that are alive from the dead,' and their members as 'instruments of righteousness unto God' (Rom. 6:13). This is the demand which He makes upon us: to *be* our *God*, to be served as such by us; for us to be and do, absolutely and without reserve, whatsoever He demands, surrendering ourselves fully to Him (see Luke 14:26, 27, 33). It belongs to God as God to legislate, prescribe, determine for us; it belongs to us as a bounden duty to be ruled, governed, disposed of by Him at His pleasure.

To own God as our God is to give Him the throne of our hearts. It is to say in the language of Isaiah 26:13, 'O Lord our God, other lords beside thee have had dominion over us: but by thee *only* will we make mention of thy name.' It is to declare with the Psalmist, not hypocritically, but sincerely, 'O God, thou art my God; early will I seek thee' (Psa. 63:1). Now it is in proportion as this becomes our actual experience that we profit from the Scriptures. It is in them, and in them alone, that the claims of God are revealed and enforced, and just so far as we are obtaining clearer and fuller views of God's rights, and are *yielding ourselves* thereto, are we really being blessed.

2. *A greater fear of God's majesty.* 'Let all the earth fear the Lord; let all the inhabitants of the world stand in awe of him' (Psa. 33:8). God is so high above us that the

thought of His majesty should make us tremble. His power is so great that the realization of it ought to terrify us. He is so ineffably holy, and His abhorrence of sin is so infinite, that the very thought of wrongdoing ought to fill us with horror. 'God is greatly to be feared in the assembly of the saints, and to be had in reverence of all them that are about him' (Psa. 89:7).

'The fear of the Lord is the beginning of wisdom' (Prov. 9:10), and 'wisdom' is a right use of 'knowledge.' Just so far as God is *truly* known will He be duly feared. Of the wicked it is written, 'There is *no* fear of God before their eyes' (Rom. 3:18). They have no realization of His majesty, no concern for His authority, no respect for His commandments, no alarm that He shall judge them. But concerning His covenant people God has promised, 'I will put my fear in their hearts, that they shall not depart from me' (Jer. 32:40). Therefore do they tremble at His Word (Isa. 66:5), and walk softly before Him.

'The fear of the Lord is to hate evil' (Prov. 8:13). And again, 'By the fear of the Lord men depart from evil' (Prov. 16:6). The man who lives in the fear of God is conscious that 'the eyes of the Lord are in every place, beholding the evil and the good' (Prov. 15:3), therefore is he conscientious about his private conduct as well as his public. The one who is deterred from committing certain sins because the eyes of men are upon him, and who hesitates not to commit them when alone, is destitute of the fear of God. So too the man who moderates his language when Christians are about him, but does not so at other times, is devoid of God's fear. He has no awe-inspiring consciousness that God sees and hears him at *all* times. The truly regenerate soul is *afraid* of disobeying and defying God. Nor does he want to. No, his real and deepest desire is to *please Him* in all things, at all times, and in all places. His earnest prayer is 'Unite my heart to fear thy name' (Psa. 86:11).

Now even the saint has to be *taught* the fear of God (Psa. 34:11). And here, as ever, it is through the Scriptures that this teaching is given us (Prov. 2:5). It is through them we learn that God's eye is ever upon us, marking our actions, weighing our motives. As the Holy Spirit applies the Scriptures to our hearts, we give increasing heed to that command, 'Be thou in the fear of the Lord all the day long' (Prov. 23.17). Thus, just so far as we are awed by God's awful majesty, are made conscious that 'Thou God seest me' (Gen. 16:13), and work out our salvation with 'fear and trembling' (Phil. 2:12), are we truly profited from our reading and study of the Bible.

3. *A deeper reverence for God's commandments.* Sin entered this world by Adam's breaking of God's law, and all his fallen children are begotten in his depraved likeness (Gen. 5:3). 'Sin is the transgression of the law' (1 John 3:4). Sin is a species of high treason, spiritual anarchy. It is the repudiation of God's dominion, the setting aside of His authority, rebellion against His will. Sin is having our own way. Now salvation is deliverance from sin, from its guilt, from its power as well as its penalty. The same Spirit who convicts of the need of God's grace also convicts of the need of God's government to rule us. God's promise to His covenant people is, 'I will put my laws into their mind, and write them in their hearts: and I will be to them a God' (Heb. 8:10).

A spirit of obedience is communicated to every regenerated soul. Said Christ, 'If a man love me, he *will* keep my words' (John 14:23). There is the test: 'Hereby we do

know that we know him, if we keep his commandments'
(1 John 2:3). None of us keeps them perfectly, yet every
real Christian both desires and strives to do so. He says
with Paul, 'I delight in the law of God after the inward
man' (Rom. 7:22). He says with the Psalmist, 'I have
chosen the way of truth,' 'Thy testimonies have I *taken* as
an heritage for ever' (Psa. 119:30, 111). And teaching
which lowers God's authority, which ignores His commands, which affirms that the Christian is, in *no* sense,
under the Law, is of the Devil, no matter how oily-
mouthed his human instrument may be. Christ has redeemed His people from the curse of the Law and not from
the command of it; He has saved them from the wrath of
God, but not from His government. 'Thou shalt love the
Lord thy God with all thine heart' never has been and
never will be repealed.

1 Corinthians 9:21, expressly affirms that we *are* 'under
the law to Christ.' 'He that saith he abideth in him ought
himself so to walk, even as he walked' (1 John 2:6). And
how did Christ 'walk'? In perfect obedience to God; in
complete subjection to His law, honouring and obeying it
in thought and word and deed. He came not to destroy the
Law, but to fulfil it (Matt. 5:17). And our love for Him is
expressed, not in pleasing emotions or beautiful words, but
in keeping His commandments (John 14:15), and the
commandments of Christ are the commandments of God
(cf. Ex. 20:6). The earnest prayer of the real Christian is,
'*Make me to go* in the path of thy commandments; for
therein do I delight' (Psa. 119:35). Just so far as our reading and study of Scripture is, by the Spirit's application,
begetting within us a greater love and a deeper respect for
and a more punctual keeping of God's commandments,
are we really profiting thereby.

4. *A firmer trust in God's sufficiency.* Whatsoever or whomsoever a man most trusts in is his 'god.' Some trust in health, others in wealth; some in self, others in their friends. That which characterizes all the unregenerate is that they lean upon an arm of flesh. But the election of grace have their hearts drawn from all creature supports, to rest upon the living God. God's people are the children of faith. The language of their hearts is, 'O my God, I trust in thee: let me not be ashamed' (Psa. 25:2). and again, 'Though he slay me, yet will I trust in him' (Job 13:15). They rely upon God to provide, protect and bless them. They look to an unseen resource, count upon an invisible God, lean upon a hidden Arm.

True, there are times when their faith wavers, but though they fall they are not utterly cast down. Though it be not their uniform experience, yet Psalm 56:11 expresses the general state of their souls: 'In God have I put my trust: I will not be afraid what man can do unto me.' Their earnest prayer is, 'Lord, increase our faith.' 'Faith cometh by hearing, and hearing by the word of God' (Rom. 10:17). Thus, as the Scriptures are pondered, their promises received in the mind, faith is strengthened, confidence in God increased, assurance deepened. By this we may discover whether or not we are profiting from our study of the Bible.

5. *A fuller delight in God's perfections.* That in which a man most delights is his 'god'. The poor worldling seeks satisfaction in his pursuits, pleasures and possessions. Ignoring the Substance, he vainly pursues the shadows. But the Christian delights in the wondrous perfections of God. Really to own God as *our* God is not only to submit to His sceptre, but is to love Him more than the world, to value Him above everything and everyone else. It is to have with

the Psalmist an experiential realization that '*all* my springs are in thee' (Psa. 87:7). The redeemed have not only received a joy from God such as this poor world cannot impart, but they 'rejoice *in* God' (Rom. 5:11); and of this the poor worldling knows nothing. The language of such is 'the Lord is *my portion*' (Lam. 3:24).

Spiritual exercises are irksome to the flesh. But the real Christian says, 'It is *good* for me to draw near to God' (Psa. 73:28). The carnal man has many cravings and ambitions; the regenerate soul declares, '*One* thing have I desired of the Lord, that will I seek after; that I may dwell in the house of the Lord all the days of my life, to behold the beauty of the Lord' (Psa. 27:4). And why? Because the true sentiment of his heart is, 'Whom have I in heaven but thee? and there is none upon earth that I desire beside thee' (Psa. 73:25). Ah, my reader, if your heart has not been drawn out to love and *delight in* God, then it is still dead toward Him.

The language of the saints is, 'Although the fig tree shall not blossom, neither shall fruit be in the vines; the labour of the olive shall fail, and the fields shall yield no meat; the flock shall be cut off from the fold, and there shall be no herd in the stalls: *yet* I will rejoice in the Lord, I will joy in the God of my salvation' (Hab. 3:17, 18). Ah, that is a supernatural experience indeed! Yes, the Christian can rejoice when all his worldly possessions are taken from him (see Heb. 10:34). When he lies in a dungeon with back bleeding, he can still sing praises to God (see Acts 16:25). Thus, to the extent that you are being weaned from the empty pleasures of this world, are learning that there is no blessing outside of God, are discovering that He is the source and sum of all excellency, and your heart is being drawn out to Him, your mind stayed on Him, your soul finding its joy and satisfaction in Him, are you really profiting from the Scriptures.

6. *A larger submission to God's providences.* It is natural to murmur when things go wrong, it is supernatural to hold our peace (Lev. 10:3). It is natural to be disappointed when our plans miscarry, it is supernatural to bow to *His* appointments. It is natural to want our own way, it is supernatural to say, 'Not my will, but thine be done.' It is natural to rebel when a loved one is taken from us by death, it is supernatural to say from the heart, 'The Lord gave, and the Lord hath taken away; *blessed be* the name of the Lord' (Job 1:21). As God is truly made our portion, we learn to admire His wisdom, and to know that He does all things well. Thus the heart is kept in 'perfect peace' as the mind is stayed on Him (Isaiah 26:3). Here, then, is another sure test: if your Bible study is teaching you that *God's* way is best, if it is causing you to submit unrepiningly to all His dispensations, if you are enabled to give thanks for *all* things (Eph. 5:20), then are you profiting indeed.

7. *A more fervent praise for God's goodness.* Praise is the outflow of a heart which finds its satisfaction in God. The language of such a one is, 'I will bless the Lord at all times: his praise shall continually be in my mouth' (Psa. 34:1). What abundant cause have God's people for praising Him! Loved with an everlasting love, made sons and heirs, all things working together for their good, their every need supplied, an eternity of bliss assured them, their harps of gladness ought never to be silent. Nor will they be while they enjoy fellowship with Him who is 'altogether lovely.' The more we are 'increasing in the knowledge of God' (Col. 1:10), the more shall we adore Him. But it is only as the Word dwells in us richly that we are

filled with spiritual songs (Col. 3:16) and make melody in our hearts to the Lord. The more our souls are drawn out in true worship, the more we are found thanking and praising our great God, the clearer evidence we give that our study of His word is profiting us.

3: *The Scriptures and Christ*

THE order we follow in this series is that of *experience*. It is not until man is made thoroughly displeased with himself that he begins to aspire after God. The fallen creature, deluded by Satan, is self-satisfied till his sin-blinded eyes are opened to get a sight of himself. The Holy Spirit first works in us a sense of our ignorance, vanity, poverty and depravity, before He brings us to perceive and acknowledge that in God alone are to be found true wisdom, real blessedness, perfect goodness and unspotted righteousness. We must be made conscious of our imperfections ere we can really appreciate the Divine perfections. As the perfections of God are contemplated, man becomes still more aware of the infinite distance that separates him from the most High. As he learns something of God's pressing claims upon him, and his own utter inability to meet them, he is prepared to hear and welcome the good news that Another has fully met those claims for all who are led to believe in Him.

'Search the Scriptures,' said the Lord Jesus, and then He added, 'for . . . they are they which testify of me' (John 5:39). They testify of Him as the only Saviour for perishing sinners, as the only Mediator between God and men, as the only one through whom the Father can be approached. They testify to the wondrous perfections of His person, the varied glories of His offices, the sufficiency of His finished work. Apart from the Scriptures, He cannot be known. In them alone He is revealed. When the Holy Spirit takes of the things of Christ and shows them unto His people, in thus making them known to the soul He uses naught but what is written. While it is true that Christ is the key to the Scriptures, it is equally true that only in the Scriptures do we have an opening-up of the 'mystery of Christ' (Eph. 3:4).

Now the measure in which we profit from our reading and study of the Scriptures may be ascertained by the extent to which *Christ* is becoming more real and more precious unto our hearts. To 'grow in grace' is defined as 'and in the knowledge of our Lord and Saviour Jesus Christ' (2 Pet. 3:18): the second clause there is not something in addition to the first, but is an explanation of it. To 'know' Christ (Phil. 3:10) was the supreme longing and aim of the apostle Paul, a longing and an aim to which he subordinated all other interests. But mark it well, the 'knowledge' which is spoken of in these verses is not intellectual but spiritual, not theoretical but experimental, not general but personal. It is a supernatural knowledge, which is imparted to the regenerate heart by the operations of the Holy Spirit, as He interprets and applies to us the Scriptures concerning Him.

Now the knowledge of Christ which the blessed Spirit imparts to the believer through the Scriptures profits him in different ways, according to his varying frames, circumstances and needs. Concerning the bread which God gave to the children of Israel during their wilderness wanderings, it is recorded that 'some gathered more, some less' (Ex. 16:17). The same is true in our apprehension of Him of whom the manna was a type. There is that in the wondrous person of Christ which is exactly suited to our every condition, every circumstance, every need, both for time and eternity; but we are slow to realize it, and slower still to act upon it. There is an inexhaustible fulness in Christ (John 1:16) which is available for us to draw from, and the principle regulating the extent to which we become 'strong in the grace that is in Christ Jesus' (2 Tim. 2:1) is 'According to your faith be it to you' (Matt. 9:29).

1. An individual is profited from the Scriptures when they reveal to him *his need of Christ*. Man in his natural estate deems himself self-sufficient. True, he has a dim perception that all is not quite right between himself and God, yet has he no difficulty in persuading himself that he is able to do that which will propitiate Him. That lies at the foundation of all man's religion, begun by Cain, in whose 'way' (Jude 11) the multitudes still walk. Tell the devout religionist that 'they that are in the flesh cannot please God' (Rom. 8:8), and he is at once offended. Press upon him the fact that 'all our righteousnesses are as filthy rags' (Isa. 64:4), and his hypocritical urbanity at once gives place to anger. So it was when Christ was on earth. The most religious people of all, the Jews, had no sense that *they* were 'lost' and in dire need of an almighty Saviour.

'They that are whole need not a physician, but they that are sick' (Matt. 9:12). It is the peculiar office of the Holy Spirit, by His application of the Scriptures, to convict sinners of their desperate condition, to bring them to see that their state is such that 'from the sole of the foot even unto the head there is no soundness' in them, but 'wounds, and bruises, and putrifying sores' (Isa. 1:6). As the Spirit convicts us of our sins – our ingratitude to God, our murmuring against Him, our wanderings from Him – as He presses upon us the claims of God – His right to our love, obedience and adoration – and all our sad failures to render Him His due, then we are made to recognize that Christ is our only hope, and that, except we flee to Him for refuge, the righteous wrath of God will most certainly fall upon us.

Nor is this to be limited to the initial experience of conversion. The more the Spirit deepens His work of grace in the regenerated soul, the more that individual is made conscious of his pollution, his sinfulness and his vileness; and the more does he discover his need of and learn to value that precious, precious blood which cleanses from all sin. The Spirit is here to glorify Christ, and one chief way in which He does so is by opening wider and wider the eyes of those for whom He died, to see how suited Christ is for such wretched, foul, hell-deserving creatures. Yes, the more we are truly profiting from our reading of the Scriptures, the more do we feel our need of Him.

2. An individual is profited from the Scriptures when they *make Christ more real* to him. The great mass of the Israelitish nation saw nothing more than the outward shell in the rites and ceremonies which God gave them, but a regenerated remnant were privileged to behold Christ Himself. 'Abraham rejoiced to see my day' said Christ (John 8:56). Moses esteemed 'the reproach of Christ' greater riches than the treasures of Egypt (Heb. 11:26). So it is in Christendom. To the multitudes Christ is but a name, or at most a historical character. They have no personal dealings with Him, enjoy no spiritual communion with Him. Should they hear one speak in rapture of His excellency they regard him as an enthusiast or a fanatic. To them Christ is unreal, vague, intangible. But with the real Christian it is far otherwise. The language of his heart is,

I have heard the voice of Jesus,
Tell me not of aught beside;
I have seen the face of Jesus,
And my soul is satisfied.

Yet such a blissful sight is not the consistent and un-varying experience of the saints. Just as clouds come in between the sun and the earth, so failures in our walk inter-rupt our communion with Christ and serve to hide from us the light of His countenance. 'He that hath my command-ments, and keepeth them, he it is that loveth me: and he that loveth me shall be loved of my Father, and I will love him, and will *manifest* myself to him' (John 14:21). Yes, it is the one who by grace is treading the path of obedience to whom the Lord Jesus grants manifestations of Himself. And the more frequent and prolonged these manifestations are, the more real He becomes to the soul, until we are able to say with Job, 'I have heard of thee by the hearing of the ear; *but now* mine eye seeth thee' (42:5). Thus the more Christ is becoming a living reality to me, the more I am profiting from the Word.

3. An individual is profited from the Scriptures when he becomes *more engrossed with Christ's perfections*. It is a sense of need which first drives the soul to Christ, but it is the realization of His excellency which draws us to run after Him. The more real Christ becomes to us, the more are we attracted by His perfections. At the beginning He is viewed only as a Saviour, but as the Spirit continues to take of the things of Christ and show them unto us we dis-cover that upon His head are 'many crowns' (Rev. 19:12). Of old it was said, 'His name shall be called Wonderful' (Isa. 9:6). His name signifies all that He is as made known in Scripture. 'Wonderful' are His offices, in their number,

37

variety, sufficiency. He is the Friend that sticks closer than a brother, to help in every time of need. He is the great High Priest, who is touched with the feeling of our infirmities. He is the Advocate with the Father, who pleads our cause when Satan accuses us.

Our great need is to be occupied with Christ, to sit at His feet as Mary did, and receive out of His fulness. Our chief delight should be to 'consider the Apostle and High Priest of our profession' (Heb. 3:1): to contemplate the various relations which He sustains to us, to meditate upon the many promises He has given, to dwell upon His wondrous and changeless love for us. As we do this, we shall so delight ourselves in the Lord that the siren voices of this world will lose all their charm for us. Ah, my reader, do you know anything about this in your own actual experience? Is Christ the chief among ten thousand to your soul? Has He won your heart? Is it your chief joy to get alone and be occupied with Him? If not, your Bible reading and study has profited you little indeed.

4. An individual is profited from the Scriptures as *Christ becomes more precious* to him. Christ is precious in the esteem of all true believers (1 Pet. 2:7). They count all things but loss for the excellency of the knowledge of Christ Jesus their Lord (Phil. 3:8). His name to them is as ointment poured forth (Song of Sol. 1:3). As the glory of God that appeared in the wondrous beauty of the temple, and in the wisdom and splendour of Solomon, drew worshippers to him from the uttermost parts of the earth, so the unparalleled excellency of Christ which was prefigured thereby does more powerfully attract the hearts of His people. The Devil knows this full well, therefore is he ceaselessly engaged in blinding the minds of them that believe not, by placing between them and Christ the allure-

ments of this world. God permits him to assail the believer also, but it is written, 'Resist the devil, and he will flee from you' (James 4:7). Resist him by definite and earnest prayer, entreating the Spirit to draw out your affections to Christ.

The more we are engaged with Christ's perfections, the more we love and adore Him. It is lack of experimental acquaintance with Him that makes our hearts so cold towards Him. But where real and daily fellowship is cultivated the Christian will be able to say with the Psalmist, 'Whom have I in heaven but thee? and there is none upon earth that I desire beside thee' (Psa. 73:25). This it is which is the very essence and distinguishing nature of true Christianity. Legalistic zealots may be busily engaged in tithing mint and anise and cummin, they may encompass sea and land to make one proselyte, and yet have no love for God in Christ. It is the heart that God looks at: 'My son, give me thine heart' (Prov. 23:26) is His demand. The more precious Christ is to us, the more delight does He have in us.

5. An individual who is profited from the Scriptures has an *increasing confidence in Christ*. There is 'little faith' (Matt. 14:3) and 'great faith' (Matt. 8:10). There is the 'full assurance of faith' (Heb. 10:22), and trusting in the Lord 'with all the heart' (Prov. 3:5). Just as there is growing' from strength to strength' (Psa. 84:7), so we read of 'from faith to faith' (Rom. 1:17). The stronger and steadier our faith, the more the Lord Jesus is honoured. Even a cursory reading of the four Gospels reveals the fact that nothing pleased the Saviour more than the firm reliance which was placed in Him by the few who really counted upon Him. He Himself lived and walked by faith, and the more we do so the more are the members being con-

formed to their Head. Above everything else there is one thing to be aimed at and diligently sought by earnest prayer: that our faith may be increased. Of the Thessalonian saints Paul was able to say, 'Your faith groweth exceedingly' (2 Thess. 1:3).

Now Christ cannot be trusted at all unless He be known, and the better he is known the more will He be trusted: 'And they that know thy name *will* put their trust in thee' (Psa. 9:10). As Christ becomes more real to the heart, as we are increasingly occupied with His manifold perfections and He becomes more precious to us, confidence in Him is deepened until it becomes as natural to trust Him as it is to breathe. The Christian life is a *walk* of faith (2 Cor. 5:7), and that very expression denotes a continual progress, an increasing deliverance from doubts and fears, a fuller assurance that all He has promised He will perform. Abraham is the father of all them that believe, and thus the record of his life furnishes an illustration of what a deepening confidence in the Lord signifies. First, at His bare word he turned his back upon all that was dear to the flesh. Second, he went forth in simple dependence on Him and dwelt as a stranger and sojourner in the land of promise, though he never owned a single acre of it. Third, when the promise was made of a seed in his old age, he considered not the obstacles in the way of its fulfilment, but was strong in faith, giving glory to God. Finally, when called on to offer up Isaac, through whom the promises were to be realized, he accounted that God was able to 'raise him up, even from the dead' (Heb. 11:19).

In the history of Abraham we are shown how grace is able to subdue an evil heart of unbelief, how the spirit may be victorious over the flesh, how the supernatural fruits of a God-given and God-sustained faith may be brought forth by a man of like passions with us. This is recorded for our encouragement, for us to pray that it may please the Lord to work in us what He wrought in and through the father of the faithful. Nothing more pleases, honours and glorifies Christ than the confiding trust, the expectant confidence and the childlike faith of those to whom He has given every cause to trust Him with all their hearts. And nothing more evidences that we are being profited from the Scriptures than an increasing faith in Christ.

6. An individual is profited from the Scriptures when they beget in him a *deepening desire to please Christ*. 'Ye are not your own, for ye are bought with a price' (1 Cor. 6:19, 20) is the first great fact that Christians need to apprehend. Henceforth they are not to 'live unto themselves, but unto him which died for them, and rose again' (2 Cor. 5:15). Love delights to please its object, and the more our affections are drawn out to Christ the more shall we desire to honour Him by a life of obedience to His known will. 'If a man love me, he will keep my words' (John 14:23). It is not in happy emotions or in verbal professions of devotion, but in the actual assumption of His yoke and the practical submitting to His precepts, that Christ is most honoured.

It is at this point particularly that the genuineness of our profession may be tested and proved. Have they a faith in Christ who make no effort to learn His will? What a contempt of the king if his subjects refuse to read his proclamations! Where there is faith in Christ there will be delight in His commandments, and a sorrowing when they are broken by us. When we displease Christ we should mourn over our failure. It is impossible seriously to believe that it was my sins which caused the Son of God to shed His precious blood without my hating them. If Christ groaned under sin, we shall groan too. And the more sincere those groanings be, the more earnestly shall we seek grace for deliverance from all that displeases, and strength to do all that which pleases our blessed Redeemer.

7. An individual is profited from the Scriptures when they cause him to *long for the return of Christ*. Love can be satisfied with nothing short of a sight of its object. True, even now we behold Christ by faith, yet it is 'through a glass, darkly.' But at His coming we shall behold Him 'face to face' (1 Cor. 13:12). Then will be fulfilled His own words, 'Father, I will that they also, whom thou hast given me, be with me where I am: that they may behold my glory, which thou hast given me: for thou lovedst me before the foundation of the world' (John 17:24). Only this will fully meet the longings of His heart, and only this will meet the longings of those redeemed by Him. Only then will He 'see of the travail of His soul, and be satisfied' (Isa. 53:11); and 'As for me, I will behold thy face in righteousness: I shall be satisfied, when I awake, with Thy likeness' (Psa. 17:15).

At the return of Christ we shall be done with sin for ever. The elect are predestined to be conformed to the image of God's Son, and that Divine purpose will be realized only when Christ receives His people unto Himself. 'We shall be like him, for we shall see him as he is' (1 John 3:2). Never again will our communion with Him be broken, never again shall we groan and moan over our inward corruptions; never again shall we be harrassed with unbelief. He will present His Church to Himself 'a glorious church, not having spot, or wrinkle, or any such thing' (Eph. 5:27). For that hour we eagerly wait. For our Redeemer we lovingly look. The more we yearn for the coming One, the more we are trimming our lamps in earnest expectation of His coming, the more do we give evidence that we are profiting from our knowledge of the Word.

Let the reader and writer honestly search themselves as in the presence of God. Let us seek truthful answers to these questions. Have we a deeper sense of our need of Christ? Is He Himself becoming to us a brighter and living reality? Are we finding increasing delight in being occupied with His perfections? Is Christ Himself becoming daily more precious to us? Is our faith in Him growing so that we confidently trust Him for everything? Are we really seeking to please Him in all the details of our lives? Are we so yearning for Him that we would be filled with joy did we know for certain that He would come during the next twenty-four hours? May the Holy Spirit search our hearts with these pointed questions!

4: *The Scriptures and Prayer*

Aprayerless Christian is a contradiction in terms. Just as a still-born child is a dead one, so a professing believer who does not pray is devoid of spiritual life. Prayer is the breath of the new nature in the saint, as the Word of God is its food. When the Lord would assure the Damascus disciple that Saul of Tarsus had been truly converted, He told him, 'Behold, he prayeth' (Acts 9:11). On many occasions had that self-righteous Pharisee bowed his knees before God and gone through his 'devotions,' but this was the first time he had ever really *prayed*. This important distinction needs emphasizing in this day of powerless forms (2 Tim. 3:5). They who content themselves with formal addresses to God know Him not; for 'the spirit of grace *and* supplications' (Zech. 12:10) are never separated. God has no dumb children in His regenerated family: 'Shall not God avenge his own elect, which cry day and night unto Him?' (Luke 18:7). Yes, 'cry' unto Him, not merely 'say' their prayers.

But will the reader be surprised when the writer declares it is his deepening conviction that, probably, the Lord's own people sin more in their efforts to pray than in connection with any other thing they engage in? What hypocrisy there is, where there should be reality! What presumptuous demandings, where there should be submissiveness! What formality, where there should be brokenness of heart! How little we really *feel* the sins we confess, and what little *sense* of deep need for the mercies we seek! And even where God grants a measure of deliverance from these awful sins, how much coldness of heart, how much unbelief, how much self-will and self-pleasing have we to bewail! Those who have no conscience upon these things are strangers to the spirit of holiness.

Now the Word of God should be our directory in prayer. Alas, how often we have made our own fleshly inclinations the rule of our asking. The Holy Scriptures have been given to us 'that the man of God may be perfect, throughly furnished unto all good works' (2 Tim. 3:17). Since we are required to 'pray in the Spirit' (Jude 20), it follows that our prayers ought to be according to the Scriptures, seeing that He is their Author throughout. It equally follows that according to the measure in which the Word of Christ dwells in us 'richly' (Col. 3:16) or sparsely, the more or the less will our petitions be in harmony with the mind of the Spirit, for 'out of the abundance of the heart the mouth speaketh' (Matt. 12:34). In proportion as we hide the Word in our hearts, and it cleanses, moulds and regulates our inner man, will our prayers be acceptable in God's sight. Then shall we be able to say, as David did in another connection, 'Of thine own have we given thee' (1 Chron. 29:14).

Thus the purity and power of our prayer-life are another index by which we may determine the extent to which we are profiting from our reading and searching of the Scriptures. If our Bible study is not, under the blessing of the Spirit, convicting us of the sin of prayerlessness, revealing to us the place which prayer ought to have in our daily lives, and is actually bringing us to spend more time in the secret place of the Most High; unless it is teaching us how to pray more acceptably to God, how to appropriate His promises and plead them before Him, how to appropriate His precepts and turn them into petitions, then not only has the time we spend over the Word been to little or no soul enrichment, but the very knowledge that we have acquired of its letter will only add to our condemnation in the day to come. 'Be ye doers of the word, and not hearers only, deceiving your own selves' (James 1:22) applies to its prayer-admonitions as to everything else in it. Let us now point out seven criteria.

1. We are profited from the Scriptures when we are brought to realize *the deep importance of prayer*. It is really to be feared that many present-day readers (and even students) of the Bible have no deep convictions that a definite prayer-life is absolutely essential to a daily walking and communing with God, as it is for deliverance from the power of indwelling sin, the seductions of the world, and the assaults of Satan. If such a conviction really gripped their hearts, would they not spend far more time on their faces before God? It is worse than idle to reply, 'A multitude of duties which have to be performed crowd out prayer, though much against my wishes.' But the fact remains that each of us takes time for anything we deem to be imperative. Who ever lived a busier life than our Saviour? Yet who found more time for prayer? If we truly yearn to be suppliants and intercessors before God and use all the available time we now have, He will so order things for us that we shall have more time.

The lack of positive conviction of the deep importance of prayer is plainly evidenced in the corporate life of professing Christians. God has plainly said, 'My house shall be called the house of prayer' (Matt. 21:13). Note, not 'the house of preaching and singing,' but of *prayer*. Yet, in the great majority of even so-called orthodox churches, the ministry of prayer has become a negligible quantity. There are still evangelistic campaigns, and Bible-teaching conferences, but how rarely one hears of two weeks set apart for special prayer! And how much good do these 'Bible conferences' accomplish if the prayer-life of the churches is not strengthened? But when the Spirit of God applies in power to our hearts such words as, 'Watch ye and pray, lest ye enter into temptation' (Mark 14:38), 'In every thing by prayer and supplication with thanksgiving let your requests be made known to God' (Phil. 4:6), 'Continue in prayer, and watch in the same with thanksgiving' (Col. 4:2), then are we being profited from the Scriptures.

2. We are profited from the Scriptures when we are made to feel that *we know not how to pray*. 'We know not what we should pray for as we ought' (Rom. 8:26). How very few professing Christians really believe this! The idea most generally entertained is that people know well enough what they should pray for, only they are careless and wicked, and so fail to pray for what they are fully assured is their duty. But such a conception is at direct variance with this inspired declaration in Romans 8:26. It is to be observed that that flesh-humbling affirmation is made not simply of men in general, but of the saints of God in particular, among which the apostle did not hesitate to include himself: '*We* know not what we should pray for as we ought.' If this be the condition of the regenerate, how much more so of the unregenerate! Yet it is one thing to read and mentally assent to what this verse says, but it is quite another to have an experimental realization of it, for the heart to be made to feel that what God requires from us He must *Himself* work in and through us.

> '*I often say my prayers,*
> *But do I ever pray?*
> *And do the wishes of my heart*
> *Go with the words I say?*
> *I may as well kneel down*
> *And worship gods of stone,*
> *As offer to the living God*
> *A prayer of words alone*'

It is many years since the writer was taught these lines by his mother – now 'present with the Lord' – but their searching message still comes home with force to him. The Christian can no more *pray* without the direct enabling of the Holy Spirit than he can create a world. This must be so, for real prayer is a felt need awakened within us by the Spirit, so that we ask God, in the name of Christ, for that which is in accord with His holy will. 'If we ask any thing according to his will, he heareth us' (1 John 5: 14). But to ask something which is not according to God's will is not praying, but presuming. True, God's revealed will is made known in His Word, yet not in such a way as a cookery book contains recipes and directions for preparing various dishes. The Scriptures frequently enumerate principles which call for continuous exercise of heart and Divine help to show us their application to different cases and circumstances. Thus we are being profited from the Scriptures when we are taught our deep need of crying 'Lord, *teach* us to pray' (Luke 11:1), and are actually constrained to beg Him for the spirit of prayer.

3. We are profited from the Scriptures when we are made conscious *of our need of the Spirit's help*. First, that He may make known to us our real wants. Take, for example, our temporal needs. How often we are in some external strait; things from without press hard upon us,

and we long to be delivered from these trials and difficulties. Surely *here* we 'know' of ourselves *what* to pray for. No, indeed; far from it! The truth is that, despite our natural desire for relief, so ignorant are we, so dull is our discernment, that (even where there is an exercised conscience) we know not what submission unto His pleasure God may require, or how He may sanctify these afflictions to our inward good. Therefore, God calls the petitions of most who seek for relief from external trials 'howlings,' and not a crying unto Him with the heart (see Hos. 7:14). 'For who knoweth what is good for man in this life?' (Eccles. 6:12). Ah, heavenly wisdom is needed to teach us our temporal 'needs' so as to make them a matter of prayer according to the mind of God.

Perhaps a few words need to be added to what has just been said. Temporal things *may be* scripturally prayed for (Matt. 6:11, etc.), but with this threefold limitation. First, *incidentally* and not primarily, for they are not the things which Christians are principally concerned in (Matt. 6:33). It is heavenly and eternal things (Col. 3:1) which are to be sought first and foremost, as being of far greater importance and value than temporal things. Second, *subordinately*, as a means to an end. In seeking material things from God it should not be in order that we may be gratified, but as an aid to our pleasing Him better. Third, *submissively*, not dictatorially, for that would be the sin of presumption. Moreover, we know not whether any temporal *mercy* would really contribute to our highest good (Psa. 106:18), and therefore we must leave it with God to decide.

We have inward wants as well as outward. Some of these may be discerned in the light of conscience, such as the guilt and defilement of sin, of sins against light and nature and the plain letter of the law. Nevertheless, the knowledge which we have of ourselves by means of the conscience is so dark and confused that, apart from the Spirit, we are in no way able to discover the true fountain of cleansing. The things about which believers do and ought to treat primarily with God in their supplications are the inward frames and spiritual dispositions of their souls. Thus, David was not satisfied with confessing all known transgressions and his original sin (Psa. 51:1–5), nor yet with an acknowledgment that none could understand his errors, whence he desired to be cleansed from 'secret faults' (Psa. 19:12); but he also begged God to undertake the inward searching of his heart to find out what was amiss in him (Psa. 139:23, 24), knowing that God principally requires 'truth in the inward parts' (Psa. 51:6). Thus, in view of 1 Corinthians 2:10–12, we should definitely seek the Spirit's aid that we may pray acceptably to God.

4. We are profited from the Scriptures when the Spirit teaches us *the right end in praying*. God has appointed the ordinance of prayer with at least a threefold design. First, that the great triune God might be honoured, for prayer is an act of worship, a paying homage; to the Father as the Giver, in the Son's name, by whom alone we may approach Him, by the moving and directing power of the Holy Spirit. Second, to humble our hearts, for prayer is ordained to bring us into the place of dependence, to develop within us a sense of our helplessness, by owning that without the Lord we can do nothing, and that we are beggars upon His charity for everything we are and have. But how feebly is this realized (if at all) by any of us until the Spirit takes us in hand, removes pride from us, and gives God His true place in our hearts and thoughts. Third, as a means or way of obtaining for ourselves the good things for which we ask.

It is greatly to be feared that one of the principal reasons why so many of our prayers remain unanswered is because we have a wrong, an unworthy end in view. Our Saviour said, 'Ask, and it shall be given you' (Matt. 7:7): but James affirms of some, 'Ye ask, and receive not, because ye ask amiss, that ye may consume it upon your lusts' (James 4:3). To pray for anything, and not expressly unto the end which God has designed, is to 'ask amiss,' and therefore to no purpose. Whatever confidence we may have in our own wisdom and integrity, if we are left to ourselves our aims will never be suited to the will of God. Unless the Spirit restrains the flesh within us, our own natural and distempered affections intermix themselves in our supplications, and thus are rendered vain. 'Whatsoever ye do, do all to the glory of God' (1 Cor. 10:31), yet none but the Spirit can enable us to subordinate all our desires unto God's glory.

5. We are profited from the Scriptures when we are taught *how to plead God's promises*. Prayer must be in faith (Rom. 10:14), or God will not hear it. Now faith has respect to God's promises (Heb. 4:1; Rom. 4:21); if, therefore, we do not understand what God stands pledged to give, we cannot pray at all. The promises of God contain the matter of prayer and define the measure of it. What God has promised, all that He has promised, and nothing else, we are to pray for. 'Secret things belong unto the Lord our God' (Deut. 29:29), but the declaration of His will and the revelation of His grace belong unto us, and are our rule. There is nothing that we really stand in need of but God has promised to supply it, yet in such a way and under such limitations as will make it good and useful to us. So too there is nothing God has promised but we stand in need of it, or are some way or other concerned in

it as members of the mystical body of Christ. Hence, the better we are acquainted with the Divine promises, and the more we are enabled to understand the goodness, grace and mercy prepared and proposed in them, the better equipped are we for acceptable prayer.

Some of God's promises are general rather than specific; some are conditional, others unconditional; some are fulfilled in this life, others in the world to come. Nor are we able of ourselves to discern which promise is most suited to our particular case and present emergency and need, or to appropriate by faith and rightly plead it before God. Wherefore we are expressly told, 'For what man knoweth the things of a man save the spirit of man which is in him? Even so the things of God knoweth no man, but the Spirit of God. Now we have received, not the spirit of the world but the Spirit which is of God; that we might know the things that are freely given to us of God' (1 Cor. 2:11, 12). Should someone reply, If so much be required unto acceptable praying, if we cannot supplicate God aright without much less trouble than you indicate, few will continue long in this duty, then we answer that such an objector knows not what it is to pray, nor does he seem willing to learn.

6. We are profited from the Scriptures when we are brought to *complete submission unto God*. As stated above, one of the Divine designs in appointing prayer as an ordinance is that we might be humbled. This is outwardly denoted when we bow the knee before the Lord. Prayer is an acknowledgment of our helplessness, and a looking to Him from whom all our help comes. It is an owning of His sufficiency to supply our every need. It is a making known our 'requests' (Phil. 4:6) unto God; but requests are very different from *demands*. 'The throne of grace is not set up

53

that we may come and there vent our passions before God' (Wm. Gurnall). We are to spread our case before God, but leave it to His superior wisdom to prescribe how it shall be dealt with. There must be no dictating, nor can we 'claim' anything from God, for we are beggars dependent upon His mere mercy. In all our praying we must add, 'Nevertheless, not as I will, but as thou wilt.'

But may not faith plead God's promises and expect an answer? Certainly; but it must be *God's* answer. Paul besought the Lord thrice to remove his thorn in the flesh; instead of doing so, the Lord gave him grace to endure it (2 Cor. 12). Many of God's promises are promiscuous rather than personal. He has promised His Church pastors, teachers and evangelists, yet many a local company of His saints has languished long without them. Some of God's promises are indefinite and general rather than absolute and universal; as, for example Ephesians 6:2, 3. God has not bound Himself to give in kind or specie, to grant the particular thing we ask for, even though we ask in faith. Moreover, He reserves to *Himself* the right to determine the fit time and season for bestowing His mercies. 'Seek ye the Lord, all ye meek of the earth . . . it *may be* ye shall be hid in the day of the Lord's anger' (Zeph. 2:3). Just because it 'may be' God's will to grant a certain temporal mercy unto me, it is my duty to cast myself upon Him and plead for it, yet with entire submission to His good pleasure for the performance of it.

7. We are profited from the Scriptures when prayer becomes *a real and deep joy*. Merely to 'say our prayers' each morning and evening is an irksome task, a duty to be performed which brings a sigh of relief when it is done. But really to come into the conscious presence of God, to behold the glorious light of His countenance, to commune

with Him at the mercy seat, is a foretaste of the eternal bliss awaiting us in heaven. The one who is blessed with this experience says with the Psalmist, 'It is good for me to draw near to God' (Psa. 73:28). Yes, good for the heart, for it is quietened; good for faith, for it is strengthened; good for the soul, for it is blessed. It is lack of this soul communion with God which is the root cause of our unanswered prayers: 'Delight thyself also in the Lord; and he *shall* give thee the desires of thine heart' (Psa. 37:4).

What is it which, under the blessing of the Spirit, produces and promotes this joy in prayer? First, it is the heart's delight in God as the Object of prayer, and particularly the recognition and realization of God as *our Father*. Thus, when the disciples asked the Lord Jesus to teach them to pray, He said, 'After this manner therefore pray ye: Our Father which art in heaven.' And again, 'God hath sent forth the Spirit of his Son into your hearts, crying, Abba [the Hebrew for 'Father'], Father' (Gal. 4:6), which includes a filial, holy delight in God, such as children have in their parents in their most affectionate addresses to them. So again, in Ephesians 2:18, we are told, for the strengthening of faith and the comfort of our hearts, 'For through him [Christ] we both have access by one Spirit unto *the Father*.' What peace, what assurance, what freedom this gives to the soul: to know we are approaching our Father!

Second, joy in prayer is furthered by the heart's apprehension and the soul's sight of God as on the throne of *grace* – a sight or prospect, not by carnal imagination, but by spiritual illumination, for it is by faith that we 'see him who is invisible' (Heb. 11:27); faith being the 'evidence of things not seen' (Heb. 11:1), making its proper object evident and present unto them that believe. Such a sight of

God upon such a 'throne' cannot but thrill the soul. Therefore are we exhorted, 'Let us therefore come boldly unto the throne of grace, that we may obtain mercy, and find grace to help in time of need' (Heb. 4:16).

Thirdly, and drawn from the last quoted scripture, freedom and delight in prayer are stimulated by the consciousness that God is, through Jesus Christ, willing and ready to dispense grace and mercy to suppliant sinners. There is no reluctance in Him which we have to overcome. He is more ready to give than we are to receive. So He is represented in Isaiah 30:18, 'And therefore will the Lord wait, that He may be gracious unto you.' Yes, He waits to be sought unto; waits for faith to lay hold of His readiness to bless. His ear is ever open to the cries of the righteous. Then 'let us draw near with a true heart in *full assurance of faith*' (Heb. 10:22); 'in *every thing* by prayer and supplication with thanksgiving let your requests be made known unto God,' and we shall find that peace which passes all understanding guarding our hearts and minds through Christ Jesus (Phil. 4:6, 7).

5: *The Scriptures and Good Works*

THE truth of God may well be likened to a narrow path skirted on either side by a dangerous and destructive precipice: in other words, it lies between two gulfs of error. The aptness of this figure may be seen in our proneness to sway from one extreme to another. Only the Holy Spirit's enabling can cause us to preserve the balance, failure to do which inevitably leads to a fall into error, for error is not so much the denial of truth as the perversion of truth, the pitting of one part of it against another.

The history of theology forcibly and solemnly illustrates this fact. One generation of men have rightly and earnestly contended for that aspect of truth which was most needed in their day. The next generation, instead of walking therein and moving forward, warred for it intellectually as the distinguishing mark of *their* party, and usually, in their defence of what was assaulted, have refused to listen to the balancing truth which often their opponents were insisting upon; the result being that they lost their sense of perspective and emphasized what they believed *out of its scriptural proportions*. Consequently, in the next generation, the true servant of God is called on almost to ignore what was so valuable in their eyes, and to emphasize that which they had, if not altogether denied, almost completely lost sight of.

It has been said that 'Rays of light, whether they proceed from the sun, star, or candle, move in perfect straight lines; yet so inferior are our works to God's that the steadiest hand cannot draw a perfectly straight line; nor, with all his skill, has man ever been able to invent an instrument capable of doing a thing apparently so simple' (T. Guthrie, 1867). Be this so or not, certain it is that men, left to themselves, have ever found it impossible to keep the even line of truth between what appear to be conflicting doctrines: such as the sovereignty of God and the responsibility of man; election by grace and the universal proclamation of the Gospel; the justifying faith of Paul and the justifying works of James. Only too often, where the absolute sovereignty of God has been insisted upon, it has been to the ignoring of man's accountability; and where unconditional election has been held fast, the unfettered preaching of the Gospel to the unsaved has been let slip. On the other hand, where human accountability has been upheld and an evangelical ministry been sustained, the sovereignty of God and the truth of election have generally been whittled down or completely ignored.

Many of our readers have witnessed examples which illustrate the truth of what has been said above, but few seem to realize that exactly the same difficulty is experienced when an attempt is made to show the precise relation between faith and good works. If, on the one hand, some have erred in attrributing to good works a place which Scripture does not warrant, certain it is that, on the other hand, some have failed to give to good works the province which Scripture assigns them. If, on the one side, it be serious error to ascribe our justification before God to any performances of ours, on the other side they are equally guilty who deny that good works are *necessary* in order to our reaching heaven, and allow nothing more than that they are merely evidences or fruits of our justification. We are well aware that we are now (shall we say) treading on thin ice, and running a serious risk of ourselves being charged with heresy; nevertheless we deem it expedient to seek Divine aid in grappling with this difficulty, and then commit the issues thereof to God Himself.

In some quarters the claims of faith, though not wholly denied, have been disparaged because of a zeal to magnify good works. In other circles, reputed as orthodox (and they are what we now have chiefly in mind), only too rarely are good works assigned their proper place, and far too infrequently are professing Christians urged with apostolic earnestness to maintain them. No doubt this is due at times to a fear of undervaluing faith, and encouraging sinners in the fatal error of trusting to their own doings rather than to and in the righteousness of Christ. But no such apprehensions should hinder a preacher from declaring 'all the counsel of God.' If his theme be faith in Christ, as the Saviour of the lost, let him fully set forth that truth without any modification, giving to this grace the place which the apostle gave it in his reply to the Philippian jailer (Acts 16:31). But if his subject be good works, let him be no less faithful in keeping back nothing which Scripture says thereon; let him not forget that Divine command, 'Affirm constantly, that they which have believed in God might be careful to maintain good works' (Titus 3:8).

The last-quoted scripture is the most pertinent one for these days of looseness and laxity, of worthless profession, and empty boasting. This expression 'good works' is found in the New Testament in the singular or plural number no less than thirty times; yet, from the rarity with which many preachers, who are esteemed sound in the faith, use, emphasize, and enlarge upon them, many of their hearers would conclude that those words occur but once or twice in all the Bible. Speaking to the Jews on another subject, the Lord said, 'What . . . God hath joined together, let not man put asunder' (Mark 10:9). Now in Ephesians 2:8-10, God has joined two most vital and blessed things together which ought never to be separated in our hearts and minds, yet they are most frequently parted in the modern pulpit. How many sermons are preached from the first two of these verses, which so clearly declare salvation to be by grace through faith and not of works. Yet how seldom are we reminded that the sentence which begins with grace and faith is only completed in verse 10, where we are told, 'For we are His workmanship, created in Christ Jesus unto good works, which God hath before ordained that we should walk in them.'

We began this series by pointing out that the Word of God may be taken up from various motives and read with different designs, but that 2 Timothy 3:16, 17, makes known for what these Scriptures are really 'profitable,' namely for doctrine or teaching, for reproof, correction, instruction in righteousness, and all of these that 'the man of God may be perfect, throughly furnished unto all good works.' Having dwelt upon its teaching about God and Christ, its reproofs and corrections for sin, its instruction in connection with prayer, let us now consider how these furnish us unto 'all good works.' Here is another vital criterion by which an honest soul, with the help of the Holy Spirit, may ascertain whether or not his reading and study of the Word is really benefiting him.

1. We profit from the Word when we are thereby taught

the true place of good works. 'Many persons, in their eagerness to support orthodoxy as a system, speak of salvation by grace and faith in such a manner as to undervalue holiness and a life devoted to God. But there is no ground for this in the Holy Scriptures. The same Gospel that declares salvation to be freely by the grace of God through faith in the blood of Christ, and asserts, in the strongest terms, that sinners are justified by the righteousness of the Saviour imputed to them on their believing in Him, without any respect to works of law, also assures us, that without holiness no man shall see God; that believers are cleansed by the blood of atonement; that their hearts are purified by faith, which works by love, and overcomes the world; and that the grace that brings salvation to all men, teaches those who receive it, that denying ungodliness and worldly lusts, they should live soberly, righteously, and godly in this present world. Any fear that the doctrine of grace will suffer from the most strenuous inculcation of good works on a scriptural foundation, betrays an inadequate and greatly defective acquaintance with Divine truth, and any tampering with the Scriptures in order to silence their testimony in favour of the fruits of righteousness, as *absolutely necessary* in the Christian, is a perversion and forgery with respect to the Word of God' (Alexander Carson).

But what force (ask some) has this ordination or command of God unto good works, when, notwithstanding it, though we fail to apply ourselves diligently unto obedience, we shall nevertheless be justified by the imputation of Christ's righteousness, and so may be saved without them? Such a senseless objection proceeds from utter ignorance of the believer's present state and relation to God. To suppose that the hearts of the regenerate are not as much and as effectually influenced with the authority and commands of God unto obedience as if they were given in order unto their justification is to ignore what true faith is, and what are the arguments and motives whereby the minds of Christians are principally affected and constrained. Moreover, it is to lose sight of the inseparable connection which God has made between our justification and our sanctification: to suppose that one of these may exist without the other is to overthrow the whole Gospel. The apostle deals with this very objection in Romans 6:1-3.

2. We profit from the Word when we are thereby taught the *absolute necessity of good works*. If it be written that 'without shedding of blood is no remission' (Heb. 9:22) and 'without faith it is impossible to please him' (Heb. 11:6), the Scripture of Truth also declares, 'Follow peace with all men, and *holiness*, without which no man shall see the Lord' (Heb. 12:14). The life lived by the saints in heaven is but the completion and consummation of that life which, after regeneration, they live here on earth. The difference between the two is not one of kind, but of degree. 'The path of the just is as the shining light, that shineth more and more unto the perfect day' (Prov. 4:18). If there has been no walking with God down here there will be no dwelling with God up there. If there has been no real communion with Him in time there will be none with Him in eternity. Death effects no vital change to the heart. True, at death the remainders of sin are for ever left behind by the saint, but no new nature is then imparted. If then he did not hate sin and love holiness before death, he certainly will not do so afterwards.

No one really desires to go to hell, though there are few indeed who are willing to forsake that broad road which inevitably leads there. All would like to go to heaven, but who among the multitudes of professing Christians are really willing and determined to walk that narrow way which alone leads thereto? It is at *this* point that we may discern the precise place which good works have in connection with salvation. They do not merit it, yet they are inseparable from it. They do not procure a title to heaven, yet they are among the *means* which God has appointed for His people's getting there. In no sense are good works the procuring cause of eternal life, but they are part of the means (as are the Spirit's work within us and repentance, faith and obedience by us) conducing to it. God has appointed the way wherein we must walk in order to our arriving at the inheritance purchased for us by Christ. A life of daily obedience to God is that which alone gives actual *admission* to the enjoyment of what Christ has purchased for His people – admission now by faith, admission at death or His return in full actuality.

3. We profit from the Word when we are taught thereby *the design of good works*. This is clearly made known in Matthew 5:16: 'Let your light so shine before men, that they may see your good works, and glorify your Father which is in heaven.' It is worthy of our notice that this is the *first* occurrence of the expression, and, as is generally the case, the initial mention of a thing in Scripture intimates its subsequent scope and usage. Here we learn that the disciples of Christ are to authenticate their Christian profession by the silent but vocal testimony of their lives (for 'light' makes no noise in its 'shining'), that men may see (not hear boastings about) their good works, and this that their Father in heaven may be glorified. Here, then, is their fundamental design: for the honour of God.

As the contents of Matthew 5:16 are so generally misunderstood and perverted we add a further thought thereon. Only too commonly the 'good works' are confounded with the 'light' itself, yet they are quite distinct, though inseparably connected. The 'light' is our *testimony* for Christ but of what value is this unless the life itself exemplifies it? The 'good works' are not for the directing of attention to ourselves, but to Him who has wrought them in us. They are to be of such a character and quality that even the ungodly will know they proceed from some higher source than fallen human nature. Supernatural fruit requires a supernatural root, and as this is recognized, the Husbandman is glorified thereby. Equally significant is the *last* reference to 'good works' in Scripture: 'Having your conversation honest among the Gentiles: that, whereas they speak against you as evildoers, they may by your good works, which they shall behold, glorify God in the day of visitation' (1 Pet. 2:12). Thus the first and final allusions emphasize their design: to glorify God because of His works through His people in this world.

4. We profit from the Word when we are taught thereby *the true nature of good works*. This is something concerning which the unregenerate are in entire ignorance. Judging merely from the external, estimating things only by human standards, they are quite incompetent to determine what works are good in God's esteem and what are not. Supposing that what men regard as good works God will approve of too, they remain in the darkness of their sin-blinded understandings; nor can any convince them of their error, till the Holy Spirit quickens them into newness of life, bringing them out of darkness into God's marvellous light. Then it will appear that only those are good works which are done in obedience to the will of God (Rom. 6:16), from a principle of love to Him (Heb. 10:24),

in the name of Christ (Col. 3:17), and to the glory of God by Him (1 Cor. 10:31).

The true nature of 'good works' was perfectly exemplified by the Lord Jesus. All that He did was done in obedience to His Father. He 'pleased not himself' (Rom. 15:3), but ever performed the bidding of the One who had sent Him (John 6:38). He could say, 'I do always those things that please him' (John 8:29). There were no limits to Christ's subjection to the Father's will: He 'became obedient unto death, even the death of the cross' (Phil. 2:8). So too all that He did proceeded from love to the Father and love to His neighbour. Love is the fulfilling of the Law; without love, compliance with the Law is naught but servile subjection, and that cannot be acceptable to Him who is Love. Proof that all Christ's obedience flowed from love is found in His words, '*I delight* to do thy will, O my God' (Psa. 40:8). So also all that Christ did had in view the glory of the Father: 'Father, glorify *thy* name' (John 12:28) revealed the object constantly before Him.

5. We profit from the Word when we are taught thereby *the true source of good works*. Unregenerate men are capable of performing works which in a natural and civil sense, though not in the spiritual sense, are good. They may do those things which, externally, as to matter and substance of them, are good, such as reading the Bible, attending the ministry of the Word, giving alms to the poor; yet the mainspring of such actions, their lack of godly motive, renders them as filthy rags in the sight of the thrice holy One. The unregenerate have no power to perform works in a *spiritual* manner, and therefore it is written, 'There is none that doeth good, no, not one' (Rom. 3:12). Nor are they able to: they are 'not subject to the law of God, neither indeed can be' (Rom. 8:7). Hence,

even the ploughing of the wicked is sin (Prov. 21:4). Nor are believers able to think a good thought or perform a good work of themselves (2 Cor. 3:5): it is God who works in them 'both to will and to do of his good pleasure' (Phil. 2:13).

When the Ethiopian can change his skin, and the leopard his spots, then may they also do good that are accustomed to do evil (Jer. 13:23). Men may as soon expect to gather grapes of thorns or figs of thistles, as good fruit to grow upon or good works to be performed by the unregenerate. We have first to be 'created in Christ Jesus' (Eph. 2:10), have His Spirit put within us (Gal. 4:6), and His grace implanted in our hearts (Eph. 4:7; 1 Cor. 15:10), before there is any capacity for good works. Even then we can do nothing apart from Christ (John 15:5). Often we have a will to do that which is good, yet how to perform it we know not (Rom. 7:18). This drives us to our knees, begging God to make us 'perfect in every good work,' *working in* us 'that which is well-pleasing in his sight, through Jesus Christ' (Heb. 13:21). Thus we are emptied of self-sufficiency, and brought to realize that all our springs are in God (Psa. 87:7); and thus we discover that we can do all things through Christ strengthening us (Phil. 4:13).

6. We profit from the Word when we are taught thereby *the great importance of good works*. Condensing as far as possible: 'good works' are of great importance because by them God is glorified (Matt. 5:16), by them the mouths of those who speak against us are closed (1 Pet. 2:12), by them we evidence the genuineness of our profession of faith (James 2:13–17). It is highly expedient that we '*adorn* the doctrine of God our Saviour in *all* things' (Titus 2:10). Nothing brings more honour to Christ than that those who

bear His name are found *living* constantly (by His enable-
ment) in a Christ-like way and spirit. It was not without
reason that the same Spirit who caused the apostle to preface his statement concerning Christ's coming into this
world to save sinners with 'This is a *faithful saying*,' etc.,
also moved him to write, 'This is a *faithful saying* . . . that
they which have believed in God might be careful to maintain good works' (Titus 3:8). May we indeed be 'zealous
of good works' (Titus 2:14).

7. We profit from the Word when we are taught thereby
the true scope of good works. This is so comprehensive as to
include the discharge of our duties in every relationship in
which God has placed us. It is interesting and instructive
to note the first 'good work' (as so described) in Holy
Writ, namely, the anointing of the Saviour by Mary of
Bethany (Matt. 26:10; Mark 14:6). Indifferent alike to
the blame or praise of men, with eyes only for the 'chiefest
among ten thousand,' she lavished upon Him her precious
ointment. Another woman, Dorcas (Acts 9:36), is also
mentioned as 'full of good works'; after worship comes
service, glorifying God among men and benefiting others.

'That ye might walk worthy of the Lord unto all pleasing, being fruitful in every good work' (Col. 1:10). The
bringing up (not 'dragging' up!) of children, lodging
(spiritual) strangers, washing the saints' feet (ministering
to their temporal comforts) and relieving the afflicted (1
Tim. 5:10) are spoken of as 'good works.' Unless our reading and study of the Scriptures is making us better soldiers
of Jesus Christ, better citizens of the country in which we
sojourn, better members of our earthly homes (kinder,
gentler, more unselfish), 'throughly furnished unto *all*
good works,' it is profiting us little or nothing.

6: *The Scriptures and Obedience*

ALL professing Christians are agreed, in theory at least, that it is the bounden duty of those who bear His name to honour and glorify Christ in this world. But as to *how* this is to be done, as to what He requires from us to this end, there is wide difference of opinion. Many suppose that honouring Christ simply means to join some 'church,' take part in and support its various activities. Others think that honouring Christ means to speak of Him to others and be diligently engaged in 'personal work.' Others seem to imagine that honouring Christ signifies little more than making liberal financial contributions to His cause. Few indeed realize that Christ is honoured only as we *live holily* unto Him, and that, by walking in subjection to His revealed will. Few indeed really believe that word, 'Behold, *to obey* is better than sacrifice, and *to hearken* than the fat of rams' (1 Sam. 15:22).

We are not Christians at all unless we have fully surrendered to and 'received Christ Jesus *the Lord*' (Col. 2:6). We would plead with you to ponder that statement diligently. Satan is deceiving many today by leading them to suppose that they are savingly trusting in 'the finished work' of Christ while their hearts remain unchanged and self still rules their lives. Listen to God's Word: 'Salvation is far from the wicked; *for they seek not* thy statutes' (Psa.

119:155). Do you really *seek* His statutes'? Do you diligently search His Word to discover what He has commanded? 'He that saith, I know Him, and keepeth not his commandments, is a liar, and the truth is not in him' (1 John 2:4). What could be plainer than that?

'And why call ye me, Lord, Lord, and *do not* the things which I say?' (Luke 6:46). Obedience to the Lord in life, not merely glowing words from the lips, is what Christ requires. What a searching and solemn word is that in James 1:22: 'Be ye doers of the word, and not hearers only, deceiving your own selves'! There are many 'hearers' of the Word, regular hearers, reverent hearers, interested hearers; but alas, what they hear is not *incorporated* into the life: it does not regulate their way. And *God* says that they who are not *doers* of the Word are deceiving their own selves!

Alas, how many such there are in Christendom today! They are not downright hypocrites, but deluded. They suppose that because they are so clear upon salvation by grace alone *they* are saved. They suppose that because they sit under the ministry of a man who has 'made the Bible a new book' to them they have grown in grace. They suppose that because their store of biblical knowledge has increased they are more spiritual. They suppose that the mere listening to a servant of God or reading his writings is *feeding on* the Word. Not so! We 'feed' on the Word only when we personally appropriate, masticate *and assimilate into our lives* what we hear or read. Where there is not an increasing conformity of heart and life to God's Word, then increased knowledge will only bring increased condemnation. 'And that servant, which *knew* his lord's will, and prepared not himself, neither *did* according to his will, shall be beaten with many stripes' (Luke 12:47).

'Ever learning, and never able to come to the knowledge of the truth' (2 Tim 3:7). This is one of the prominent characteristics of the 'perilous times' in which we are now living. People hear one preacher after another, attend this conference and that conference, read book after book on biblical subjects, and yet never attain unto a vital and practical acquaintance with the truth, so as to have an impression of its power and efficacy on the soul. There is such a thing as spiritual *dropsy*, and multitudes are suffering from it. The more they hear, the more they want to hear: they drink in sermons and addresses with avidity, but their lives are unchanged. They are puffed up with their knowledge, not humbled into the dust before God. The faith of God's elect is 'the acknowledging [in the life] of the truth which is *after godliness*' (Titus 1:1), but to this the vast majority are total strangers.

God has given us His Word not only with the design of instructing us, but for the purpose of *directing* us: to make known what He requires us to *do*. The first thing we need is a clear and distinct *knowledge* of our duty; and the first thing God demands of us is a conscientious *practice* of it, corresponding to our knowledge. 'What doth the Lord require of thee, but to do justly, and to love mercy, and to walk humbly with thy God?' (Micah 6:8). 'Let us hear the conclusion of the whole matter: Fear God, and keep his commandments: for this is the whole duty of man' (Eccles. 12:13). The Lord Jesus affirmed the same thing when He said, 'Ye are my friends, if ye do whatsoever I command you' (John 15:14).

1. A man profits from the Word as he discovers *God's demands upon him*; His undeviating demands, for *He* changes not. It is a great and grievous mistake to suppose that in this present dispensation God has *lowered* His de-

mands, for that would necessarily imply that His previous demand was a harsh and unrighteous one. Not so! 'The law is holy, and the commandment holy, and just, and good' (Rom. 7:12). The sum of God's demands is, 'Thou shalt love the Lord thy God with all thine heart, and with all thy soul, and with all thy might' (Deut. 6:5); and the Lord Jesus repeated it in Matthew 22:37. The apostle Paul enforced the same when he wrote, 'If any man *love not* the Lord Jesus Christ let him be *Anathema*' (1 Cor. 16:22).

2. A man profits from the Word when he discovers *how entirely and how sinfully he has failed to meet* God's *demands*. And let us point out for the benefit of any who may take issue with the last paragraph that no man can see what a sinner he is, how infinitely short he has fallen of measuring up to God's standard, until he has a clear sight of the exalted demands of God upon him! Just in proportion as preachers *lower* God's standard of what He requires from every human being, to that extent will their hearers obtain an inadequate and faulty conception of their sinfulness, and the less will they perceive their need of an almighty Saviour. But once a soul really perceives what are God's demands upon him, and how completely and constantly he has failed to render Him His due, then does he recognize what a desperate situation he is in. The law must be preached before any are ready for the Gospel.

3. A man profits from the Word when he is taught therefrom that *God, in His infinite grace, has fully provided for His people's meeting His own demands*. At this point, too, much present-day preaching is seriously defective. There is being given forth what may loosely be termed a 'half Gospel,' but which in reality is virtually *a denial* of the true Gospel. Christ is brought in, yet only as a sort of

make-weight. That Christ has vicariously met every demand of God upon all who believe upon Him is blessedly true, yet it is only a part of the truth. The Lord Jesus has not only vicariously satisfied for His people the requirements of God's righteousness, but He has also secured that *they* shall *personally* satisfy them too. Christ has procured the Holy Spirit to make good in them what the Redeemer wrought for them.

The grand and glorious miracle of salvation is that the saved are *regenerated*. A transforming work is wrought within them. Their understandings are illuminated, their hearts are changed, their wills are renewed. They are made 'new creatures in Christ Jesus' (2 Cor. 5:17). God refers to this miracle of grace thus: 'I will put my *laws* into their mind, and write them in their hearts' (Heb. 8:10). The heart is now inclined to God's law: a disposition has been communicated to it which *answers* to its demands; there is a sincere desire to perform it. And thus the quickened soul is able to say, 'When thou saidst, *Seek ye* my face; my heart said unto thee, thy face, Lord, *will I* seek' (Psa. 27:8).

Christ not only rendered a perfect obedience unto the Law for the justification of His believing people, but He also merited for them those supplies of His Spirit which were essential unto their sanctification, and which alone could transform carnal creatures and enable them to render acceptable obedience unto God. Though Christ died for the 'ungodly' (Rom. 5:6), though He *finds* them ungodly (Rom. 4:5) when He justifies them, yet He does not *leave them* in that abominable state. On the contrary, He effectually teaches them by His Spirit to *deny* ungodliness and worldly lusts (Titus 2:12). Just as weight cannot be separated from a stone, or heat from a fire, so cannot justification from sanctification.

When God really pardons a sinner in the court of his

conscience, under the sense of that amazing grace the heart is purified, the life is rectified, and the whole man is sanctified. Christ 'gave himself for us, that he might redeem us *from* all iniquity, and *purify* unto himself a peculiar people [not 'careless about' but], zealous of good works' (Titus 2:14). Just as a substance and its properties, causes and their necessary effects are inseparably connected, so are a saving faith *and* conscientious obedience unto God. Hence we read of 'the obedience of faith' (Rom. 16:26).

Said the Lord Jesus, 'He that hath my commandments, and keepeth them, he it is that loveth me' (John 14:21). Not in the Old Testament, the Gospels or the Epistles does God own anyone as a lover of Him save the one who keeps His commandments. Love is something more than sentiment or emotion; it is a principle of action, and it expresses itself in something more than honeyed expressions, namely, by deeds which please the object loved. 'For this is the love of God, that we keep his commandments' (1 John 5:3). Oh, my reader, you are deceiving yourself if you think you love God and yet have no deep desire and make no real effort to walk obediently before Him.

But what is obedience to God? It is far more than a mechanical performance of certain duties. I may have been brought up by Christian parents, and under them acquired certain moral habits, and yet my abstaining from taking the Lord's name in vain, and being guiltless of stealing, may be no obedience to the third and eighth commandments. Again, obedience to God is far more than conforming to the conduct of His people. I may board in a home where the Sabbath is strictly observed, and out of respect for them, or because I think it is a good and wise course to rest one day in seven, I may refrain from all unnecessary labour on that day, and yet not keep the fourth commandment at all! Obedience is not only subjection to an external law, but it is the surrendering of my will to the authority of another. Thus, obedience to God is the heart's recognition of His lordship: of His right to command, and my duty to comply. It is the complete subjection of the soul to the blessed yoke of Christ.

That obedience which God requires can proceed only from a heart which *loves* Him. 'Whatsoever ye do, do it *heartily*, as to the Lord' (Col. 3:23). That obedience which springs from a dread of punishment is servile. That obedience which is performed in order to procure favours from God is selfish and carnal. But spiritual and acceptable obedience is cheerfully given: it is the heart's free response to and gratitude for the unmerited regard and love of God for us.

4. We profit from the Word when we not only see it is our bounden duty to obey God, but *when there is wrought in us a love for His commandments*. The 'blessed' man is the one whose '*delight* is in the law of the Lord' (Psa.1:2).And again we read, 'Blessed is the man that feareth the Lord, that delighteth greatly in his commandments' (Psa. 112:1). It affords a real test for our hearts to face honestly the questions, Do I really value His 'commandments' as much as I do His *promises*? Ought I not to do so? Assuredly, for the one proceeds as truly from *His love* as does the other. The heart's compliance with the voice of Christ is the foundation for all practical holiness.

Here again we would earnestly and lovingly beg the reader to attend closely to this detail. Any man who supposes that he is saved and yet has no genuine love for God's commandment is deceiving himself. Said the Psalmist, 'O how love I thy law!' (Psa. 119:97). And again,

'Therefore I love thy commandments above gold; yea, above fine gold' (Psa. 119:127). Should someone object that *that* was under the Old Testament, we ask, Do you intimate that the Holy Spirit produces a lesser change in the hearts of those whom He now regenerates than He did of old? But a New Testament saint also placed on record, 'I *delight* in the law of God after the inward man' (Rom. 7:22). And, my reader, unless *your* heart *delights* in the 'law of God' there is something radically wrong with you; yea, it is greatly to be feared that you are spiritually dead.

5. A man profits from the Word when his heart and will are yielded to *all* God's commandments. Partial obedience is no obedience at all. A holy mind declines whatsoever God forbids, and chooses to practise all He requires, without any exception. If our minds submit not unto God in all His commandments, we submit not to *His* authority in anything He enjoins. If we do not approve of our duty in its *full* extent, we are greatly mistaken if we imagine that we have any *liking* unto *any* part of it. A person who has no principle of holiness in him may yet be disinclined to many vices and be pleased to practise many virtues, as he perceives the former are unfit actions and the latter are, in themselves, comely actions, but his disapprobation of vice and approbation of virtue do not arise from any disposition to *submit to the will of God*.

True spiritual obedience is *impartial*. A renewed heart does not pick and choose from God's commandments: the man who does so is not performing *God's* will, but his own. Make no mistake upon this point; if we do not sincerely desire to please God in *all* things, then we do not truly wish to do so in anything. Self must be denied; not merely some of the things which may be craved, but self itself! A wilful allowance of *any* known sin breaks the whole law

(James 2:10, 11). 'Then shall I not be ashamed, when I have respect unto all thy commandments' (Psa. 119:6). Said the Lord Jesus, 'Ye are my friends, if ye do *whatsoever* I command you' (John 15:14): if I am not His friend, then I must be His *enemy*, for there is no other alternative – see Luke 19:27.

6. We profit from the Word when the soul is moved to *pray earnestly for enabling grace*. In regeneration the Holy Spirit communicates a nature which is fitted for obedience according to the Word. The heart has been won by God. There is now a deep and sincere desire to please Him. But the new nature possesses no inherent power, and the old nature or 'flesh' strives against it, and the Devil opposes. Thus, the Christian exclaims, 'To will is present with me; but how to *perform* that which is good I find not' (Rom. 7:18). This does not mean that he is the slave of sin, as he was before conversion; but it means that he finds not how *fully* to realize his spiritual aspirations. Therefore does he pray, '*Make me to go* in the path of Thy commandments; for therein do I delight' (Psa. 119:35). And again, 'Order my steps in Thy word, and let not any iniquity have dominion over me' (Psa. 119:133).

Here we would reply to a question which the above statements have probably raised in many minds: Are you affirming that God requires *perfect* obedience from us in this life? We answer, Yes! God will not set any lower standard before us than that (see 1 Pet. 1:15). Then does the real Christian measure up to that standard? Yes and no! Yes, *in his heart*, and it is at *the heart* that God looks (1 Sam. 16:7). In his heart every regenerated person has a real love for God's commandments, and genuinely *desires* to keep all of them completely. It is in *this* sense, and this alone, that the Christian is experimentally 'perfect.' The

77

word 'perfect,' both in the Old Testament (Job 1:1, and Psa. 37:37) and in the new Testament (Phil. 3:15), means 'upright', 'sincere', in contrast with 'hypocritical'.

'Lord, thou hast heard the desire of the humble' (Psa. 10:17). The 'desires' of the saint are the language of his soul, and the promise is, 'He will fulfil the desire of them that fear him' (Psa. 145:19). The Christian's desire is to obey God in all things, to be completely conformed to the image of Christ. But this will only be realized in the resurrection. Meanwhile, God for Christ's sake graciously accepts the will for the deed (1 Pet. 2:5). He knows our hearts and see in His child a genuine love for and a sincere desire *to keep* all His commandments, and He accepts the fervent longing and cordial endeavour in lieu of an exact performance (2 Cor. 8:12). But let none who are living in wilful disobedience draw false peace and pervert to their own destruction what has just been said for the comfort of those who *are* heartily desirous of seeking to please God in all the details of their lives.

If any ask, How am I to know that my 'desires' are really those of a regenerate soul? we answer, Saving grace is the communication to the heart of an habitual *disposition unto* holy acts. The 'desires' of the reader are to be tested thus: Are they constant and continuous, or only by fits and starts? Are they earnest and serious, so that you really hunger and thirst after righteousness' (Matt 5:6) and pant 'after God' (Psa. 42:1)? Are they operative and efficacious? Many desire to escape from hell, yet their desires are not sufficiently strong to bring them to hate and turn from that which must inevitably bring them to hell, namely, wilful sinning against God. Many desire to go to heaven, but not so that they enter upon and follow that 'narrow way' which alone leads there. True spiritual 'desires' *use* the means of grace and spare no pains to realize them, and continue prayerfully pressing forward unto the mark set before them.

7. We profit from the Word when we are, even now, *enjoying the reward of obedience*. 'Godliness is profitable unto all things' (1 Tim. 4:8). By obedience we purify our souls (1 Pet. 1:21). By obedience we obtain the ear of God (1 John 3:22), just as disobedience is a barrier to our prayers (Isa. 59:2; Jer. 5:25). By obedience we obtain precious and intimate manifestations of Christ unto the soul (John 14:21). As we tread the path of wisdom (complete subjection to God) we discover that 'her ways are ways of pleasantness, and all her paths are peace' (Prov. 3:17). 'His commandments are *not* grievous' (1 John 5:3), and 'in keeping of them there is great reward' (Psa. 19:11).

7: *The Scriptures and the World*

Nᴏᴛ a little is written to the Christian in the New Testament about 'the world' and his attitude towards it. Its real nature is plainly defined, and the believer is solemnly warned against it. God's holy Word is a light from heaven, shining here 'in a dark place' (2 Pet. 1:19). Its Divine rays exhibit things in their true colours, penetrating and exposing the false veneer and glamour by which many objects are cloaked. That world upon which so much labour is bestowed and money spent, and which is so highly extolled and admired by its blinded dupes, is declared to be 'the enemy of God'; therefore are His children forbidden to be 'conformed' to it and to have their affections set upon it.

The present phase of our subject is by no means the least important of those that we have set out to consider, and the serious reader will do well to seek Divine grace to measure himself or herself by it. One of the exhortations which God has addressed to His children runs, 'As newborn babes, desire the sincere milk of the word, that ye may *grow* thereby' (1 Pet. 2:2), and it behoves each one of them honestly and diligently to examine himself so as to discover whether or not this be the case with him. Nor are we to be content with an increase of mere head-knowledge of Scripture: what we need to be most concerned about is our *practical* growth, our experimental conformity to the image of Christ. And one point at which we may test ourselves is, Does my reading and study of God's Word make me less worldly?

1. We profit from the Word when our eyes are opened to *discern the true character of the world*. One of the poets wrote, 'God's in His heaven – all's right with the world'. From one standpoint that is blessedly true, but from another it is radically wrong, for 'the whole world lieth in wickedness' (1 John 5:19). But it is only as the heart is supernaturally enlightened by the Holy Spirit that we are enabled to perceive that that which is highly esteemed among men is really 'abomination in the sight of God' (Luke 16:15). It is much to be thankful for when the soul is able to see that the 'world' is a gigantic fraud, a hollow bauble, a vile thing, which must one day be burned up.

Before we go further, let us define that 'world' which the Christian is forbidden to love. There are few words found upon the pages of Holy Writ used with a greater variety of meanings than this one. Yet careful attention to the context will usually determine its scope. The 'world' is a system or order of things, complete in itself. No foreign element is suffered to intrude, or if it does it is speedily accommodated or assimilated to itself. The 'world' is fallen human nature acting itself out in the human family, fashioning the framework of human society in accord with its own tendencies. It is the organized kingdom of the 'carnal mind' which is 'enmity against God' and which is 'not subject to the law of God, neither indeed can be' (Rom. 8:7). Wherever the 'carnal mind' is, there is 'the world'; so that worldliness is the world without God.

2. We profit from the Word when we learn that the world is *an enemy to be resisted and overcome*. The Christian is bidden to 'fight the good fight of faith' (1 Tim. 6:12),

which implies that there are foes to be met and vanquished. As there is the Holy Trinity – the Father, the Son, and the Holy Spirit – so also is there an evil trinity – the flesh, the world, and the Devil. The child of God is called to engage in a mortal combat with them; 'mortal', we say, for either they will destroy him or he will get the victory over them. Settle it, then, in your mind, my reader, that the world is a deadly enemy, and if you do not vanquish it in your heart then you are no child of God, for it is written 'Whatsoever is born of God *overcometh* the world' (1 John 5:4).

Out of many, the following reasons may be given as to why the world *must* be 'overcome.' First, all its alluring objects tend to divert the attention and alienate the affections of the soul from God. Necessarily so, for it is the tendency of things seen to turn the heart away from things unseen. Second, the spirit of the world is diametrically opposed to the Spirit of Christ; therefore did the apostle write, 'Now we have received, not the spirit of the world, but the Spirit which is of God' (1 Cor. 2:12). The Son of God came into the world, but 'the world knew him not' (John 1:10); therefore did its 'princes' and rulers crucify Him (1 Cor. 2:8). Third, its concerns and cares are hostile to a devout and heavenly life. Christians, like the rest of mankind, are required by God to labour six days in the week; but while so employed they need to be constantly on their guard, lest covetous *interests* govern them rather than the performance of *duty*.

'This is the victory that overcometh the world, even our faith' (1 John 5:4). Naught but a God-given faith *can* overcome the world. But as the heart is occupied with invisible yet eternal realities, it is delivered from the corrupting influence of worldly objects. The eyes of faith discern the things of sense in their real colours, and see that they are empty and vain, and not worthy to be compared with the great and glorious objects of eternity. A felt sense of the perfections and presence of God makes the world appear less than nothing. When the Christian views the Divine Redeemer dying for his sins, living to intercede for his perseverance, reigning and overruling things for his final salvation, he exclaims, 'There is none upon earth that I desire beside thee.'

And how is it with *you* as you read these lines? You may cordially assent to what has just been said in the last paragraph, but how is it with you *actually*? Do the things which are so highly valued by the unregenerate charm and enthral you? Take away from the worldling those things in which he delights, and he is wretched: is this so with you? Or, are your *present* joy and satisfaction found in objects which can *never* be taken from you? Treat not these questions lightly, we beseech you, but ponder them seriously in the presence of God. The *honest* answer to them will be an index to the real state of your soul, and will indicate whether or not you are deceived in supposing yourself to be 'a new creature in Christ Jesus.'

3. We profit from the Word when we learn that *Christ died to deliver us from 'this present evil world'* (Gal. 1:4). The Son of God came here, not only to 'fulfil' the requirements of the law (Matt. 5:17), to 'destroy the works of the devil' (1 John 3:8), to deliver us 'from the wrath to come' (1 Thess. 1:10), to save us from our sins (Matt. 1:21), but also to free us from the bondage of this world, to deliver the soul from its enthralling influence. This was foreshadowed of old in God's dealings with Israel. They were slaves in Egypt, and 'Egypt' is a figure of the world. They were in cruel bondage, spending their time in making bricks for Pharaoh. They were unable to free themselves.

But Jehovah, by His mighty power, emancipated them, and brought them forth out of the 'iron furnace.' Thus does Christ with His own. He breaks the power of the world over their hearts. He makes them independent of it, that they neither court its favours nor fear its frowns.

Christ gave Himself a sacrifice for the sins of His people that, in consequence thereof, they might be delivered from the damning power and governing influence of all that is evil in this present world: from Satan, who is its prince; from the lusts which predominate in it; from the vain conversation of the men who belong to it. And the Holy Spirit indwelling the saints co-operates with Christ in this blessed work. He turns their thoughts and affections away from earthly things to heavenly. By the working of His power, He frees them from the demoralizing influence which surrounds them, and conforms them to the heavenly standard. And as the Christian grows in grace he recognizes this, and acts accordingly. He seeks yet fuller deliverance from this 'present *evil* world,' and begs God to free him from it completely. That which once charmed him now nauseates. He longs for the time when he shall be taken out of this scene where his blessed Lord is so grievously dishonoured.

4. We profit from the Word *when our hearts are weaned from it*. 'Love not the world, neither the things that are in the world' (1 John 2:15). 'What the stumbling-block is to the traveller in the way, the weight to the runner, the lime twigs to the bird in its flight, so is the love of the world to a Christian in his course – either wholly diverting him from, greatly enticing him in, or forcibly turning him out of it' (Nathaniel Hardy, 1660). The truth is that until the heart is purged from this corruption the ear will be deaf to Divine instruction. Not until we are lifted above the

things of time and sense can we be subdued unto obedience to God. Heavenly truth glides off a carnal mind as water from a spherical body.

The world has turned its back upon Christ, and though His name is professed in many places, yet will it have nothing to do with Him. All the desires and designs of worldlings are for the gratification of *self*. Let their aims and pursuits be as varied as they may, self being supreme, everything is subordinated to the pleasing of self. Now Christians are in the world, and cannot get out of it; they have to live their Lord's appointed time in it. While here they have to earn their living, support their families, and attend to their worldly business. But they are forbidden to *love* the world, as though it could make them happy. Their 'treasure' and 'portion'are to be found elsewhere.

The world appeals to every instinct of fallen man. It contains a thousand objects to charm him: they attract his attention, the attention creates a desire for and love of them, and insensibly yet surely they make deeper and deeper impressions on his heart. It has the same fatal influence on *all* classes. But attractive and appealing as its varied objects may be, all the pursuits and pleasures of the world are designed and adapted to promote the happiness of *this life only* – therefore, 'What shall it profit a man if he should gain the whole world, and lose his own soul?' The Christian is taught by the Spirit, and through His presenting of Christ to the soul his thoughts are diverted from the world. Just as a little child will readily drop a dirty object when something more pleasing is offered to it, so the heart which is in communion with God will say, 'I count all things but loss for the excellency of the knowledge of Christ Jesus my Lord . . . and do count them but dung, that I may win Christ' (Phil. 3:8).

5. We profit from the Word *when we walk in separation from the world*. 'Know ye not that the friendship of the world is enmity with God? whosoever will be a friend of the world is the enemy of God' (James 4:4). Such a verse as this ought to search every one of us through and through, and make us tremble. How can I fraternize with or seek my pleasure in that which condemned the Son of God? If I do, that at once identifies me with His enemies. Oh, my reader, make no mistake upon this point. It is written, 'If any man love the world, the love of the Father is not in him' (1 John 2:15).

Of old it was said of the people of God that they 'shall dwell alone, and shall not be reckoned among the nations' (Num. 23:9). Surely the disparity of character and conduct, the desires and pursuits, which distinguish the regenerate from the unregenerate *must* separate the one from the other. We who profess to have our citizenship in another world, to be guided by another Spirit, to be directed by another rule, and to be journeying to another country, cannot go arm in arm with those who *despise* all such things! Then let everything in and about us exhibit the character of Christian *pilgrims*. May we indeed be 'men wondered at' (Zech. 3:8) because '*not* conformed to this world' (Rom. 12:2).

6. We profit from the Word *when we evoke the hatred of the world*. What pains are taken in the world to save appearances and keep up a seemly and good state! Its conventionalities and civilities, its courtesies and charities, are so many contrivances to give an air of respectability to it. So too its churches and cathedrals, its priests and prelates, are needed to gloss over the corruption which seethes beneath the surface. And to make good weight 'Christianity' is added, and the holy name of Christ is taken upon the lips by thousands who have never taken *His* 'yoke' upon

them. Of them God says, 'This people draweth nigh unto me with their mouth and honoureth me with their lips; but their heart is far from me' (Matt. 15:8).

And what is to be the attitude of all real Christians toward such? The answer of Scripture is plain: 'From such turn away' (2 Tim. 3:5), 'Come out from among them, and be ye separate, saith the Lord' (2 Cor. 6:17). And what will follow when this Divine command is obeyed? Why, then we shall prove the truth of those words of Christ: 'If ye were of the world, the world would love his own: but because ye are not of the world, but I have chosen you out of the world, therefore the world *hateth* you' (John 15:19). *Which* 'world' is specifically in view here? Let the previous verse answer: 'If the world hate you, ye know that it hated me before it hated you.' *What* 'world' hated Christ and hounded Him to death? The *religious* world, those who pretended to be most zealous for God's glory. So it is now. Let the Christian turn his back upon a Christ-dishonouring Christendom, and his fiercest foes and most relentless and unscrupulous enemies will be those who claim to be Christians themselves! But 'Blessed are ye, when men shall revile you, and persecute you . . . for my sake. Rejoice, and be exceeding glad' (Matt. 5:11, 12). Ah, my brother, it is a healthy sign, a sure mark that you are profiting from the Word, when the religious world hates you. But if, on the other hand, you still have a 'good standing' in the 'churches' or 'assemblies' there is grave reason to fear that you love the praise of men more than that of God!

7. We profit from the Word *when we are elevated above the world*. First, above its *customs and fashions*. The worldling is a slave to the prevailing habits and styles of the day. Not so the one who is walking with God: his chief concern

is to be 'conformed to the image of his Son.' Second, above its *cares and sorrows*: of old it was said of the saints that they took joyfully the spoiling of their goods, knowing that they had 'in heaven a better and an enduring substance' (Heb. 10:34). Third, above its *temptations*: what attraction has the glare and glitter of the world for those who are 'delighting themselves in the Lord?' None whatever! Fourth, above its *opinions and approvals*. Have you learned to be independent of and defy the world? If your whole heart is set upon pleasing God, you will be quite unconcerned about the frowns of the godless.

Now, my reader, do you really wish to measure yourself by the contents of this chapter? Then seek honest answers to the following questions. First, what are the objects before your mind in times of recreation? What do your thoughts most run upon? Second, what are the objects of your choice? When you have to decide how to spend an evening or the Sabbath afternoon, what do you select? Third, which occasions you the most sorrow, the loss of earthly things, or lack of communion with God? Which causes greater grief (or chagrin), the spoiling of your plans, or the coldness of your heart to Christ? Fourth, what is your favourite topic of conversation? Do you hanker after the news of the day, or to meet with those who talk of the 'altogether lovely' One? Fifth, do your 'good intentions' materialize, or are they nothing but empty dreams? Are you spending more or less time than formerly on your knees? Is the Word sweeter to your taste, or has your soul lost its relish for it?

8: *The Scriptures and the Promises*

THE Divine promises make known the good pleasure of God's will to His people, to bestow upon them the riches of His grace. They are the outward testimonies of His heart, who from all eternity loves them and foreappointed all things for them and concerning them. In the person and work of His Son, God has made an all-sufficient provision for their complete salvation, both for time and for eternity. To the intent that they might have a true, clear and spiritual knowledge of the same, it has pleased the Lord to set it before them in the exceeding great and precious promises which are scattered up and down in the Scriptures as so many stars in the glorious firmament of grace; by which they may be assured of the will of God in Christ Jesus concerning them, and take sanctuary in Him accordingly, and through this medium have real communion with Him in His grace and mercy at all times, no matter what their case or circumstances may be.

The Divine promises are so many declarations to bestow some good or remove some ill. As such they are a most blessed making known and manifesting of God's love to His people. There are three steps in connection with God's love: first, His inward purpose to exercise it; the last, the real execution of that purpose; but in between there is the gracious *making known* of that purpose to the beneficiaries of it. While love is concealed we cannot be comforted by it. Now God who is 'love' not only loves His own, and will not only show His love fully to them in due time, but in the interim He will have us *informed* of His benevolent designs, that we may sweetly rest in His love, and stretch ourselves comfortably upon His sure promises. There we are able to say, 'How precious also are thy thoughts unto me, O God! how great is the sum of them' (Psa. 139:17).

In 2 Peter 1:4, the Divine promises are spoken of as 'exceeding great and precious.' As Spurgeon pointed out, 'greatness and preciousness seldom go together, but in this instance they are united in an exceeding degree'. When Jehovah is pleased to open His mouth and reveal His heart He does so in a manner worthy of Himself, in words of superlative power and richness. To quote again the beloved London pastor: 'They come from a great God, they come to great sinners, they work for us great results, and deal with great matters.' While the natural intellect is capable of perceiving much of their greatness, only the renewed heart can taste their ineffable preciousness, and say with David, 'How sweet are thy words unto my taste! yea, sweeter then honey to my mouth' (Psa. 119:103).

1. We profit from the Word *when we perceive to whom the promises belong*. They are available only to those who are in Christ. 'For all the promises of God *in him* [the Lord Jesus] are yea, and in him Amen' (2 Cor. 1:20). There can be no intercourse between the thrice holy God and sinful creatures except through a Mediator who has satisfied Him on their behalf. Therefore must that Mediator receive from God all good for His people, and they must have it at second hand through Him. A sinner might just as well petition a tree as call upon God for mercy while he despises and rejects Christ.

Both the promises and the things promised are made over to the Lord Jesus and conveyed unto the saints from Him. 'This is *the* [chief and grandest] promise that he hath promised us, even eternal life' (1 John 2:25), and as the same epistle tells us, 'This life is in his Son' (5:11). This being so, what good can they who are not yet in Christ have by the promises? None at all. A man out of Christ is out of the favour of God, yea, he is under His wrath; the Divine threatenings and not the promises are *his* portion. Solemn, solemn consideration is it that those who are 'without Christ' are 'aliens from the commonwealth of Israel, and *strangers* from the covenants of promise, having *no* hope, and without God in the world' (Eph. 2:12). Only 'the children of God' are 'the children of the promise' (Rom. 9:8). Make sure, my reader, that you are one of them.

How terrible, then, is the blindness and how great is the sin of those preachers who indiscriminately apply the Divine promises to the saved and unsaved alike! They are not only taking 'the children's bread' and casting it to the 'dogs,' but they are 'handling the word of God deceitfully' (2 Cor. 4:2), and beguiling immortal souls. And they who listen to and heed them are little less guilty, for God holds all responsible to search the Scriptures for themselves, and test whatever they read or hear by that unerring standard. If they are too lazy to do so, and prefer blindly to follow their blind guides, then their blood is on their own heads. Truth has to be 'bought' (Prov. 23:23), and those who are unwilling to pay the price must go without it.

2. We profit from the Word when we *labour to make the promises of God our own*. To do this we must first take the trouble to become really acquainted with them. It is surprising how many promises there are in Scripture which the saints know nothing about, the more so seeing that *they*

are the peculiar treasure of believers, the substance of faith's heritage lying in them. True, Christians are already the recipients of wondrous blessings, yet the capital of their wealth, the bulk of their estate, is only prospective. They have already received an 'earnest,' but the better part of what Christ has purchased for them lies yet in the promise of God. How diligent, then, should they be in studying His testamentary will, familiarizing themselves with the good things which the Spirit 'hath revealed' (1 Cor. 2:10), and seeking to take an inventory of their spiritual treasures!

Not only must I search the Scriptures to find out what has been made over to me by the everlasting covenant, but I need also to meditate upon the promises, to turn them over and over in my mind, and cry unto the Lord for spiritual understanding of them. The bee would not extract honey from the flowers as long as he only gazed upon them. Nor will the Christian derive any real comfort and strength from the Divine promises until his faith lays hold of and penetrates to the heart of them. God has given no assurance that the dilatory shall be fed, but He has declared, 'the soul of the diligent shall be made fat' (Prov. 13:4). Therefore did Christ say, '*Labour* not for the meat which perisheth, but for that meat which endureth unto 'everlasting life' (John 6:27). It is only as the promises are stored up in our minds that the Spirit brings them to remembrance at those seasons of fainting when we most need them.

3. We profit from the Word when we *recognize the blessed scope of God's promises*. 'A sort of affectation prevents some Christians from seeking religion, as if its sphere lay among the commonplaces of daily life. It is to them transcendental and dreamy; rather a creation of pious fiction than a

matter of fact. They believe in God, after a fashion, for things spiritual, and for the life which is to be; but they totally forget that true godliness hath the promise of the life which now is, as well as that which is to come. To them it would seem almost profanation to pray about the small matters of which daily life is made up. Perhaps they will be startled if I venture to suggest that this should make them question the reality of their faith. If it cannot bring them help in the little troubles of life, will it support them in the greater trials of death?' (C. H. Spurgeon).

'Godliness is profitable unto all things, having *promise* of the life that *now* is, and of that which is to come' (1 Tim. 4:8). Reader, do you really believe this, that the promises of God cover *every* aspect and particular of your daily life? Or have the 'Dispensationalists' deluded you into supposing that the Old Testament belongs only to fleshly Jews, and that '*our promises*' respect spiritual and not material blessings? How many a Christian has derived comfort from 'I will never leave thee, nor forsake thee' (Heb. 13:5); well, that is a quotation from Joshua 1:5! So, too, 2 Corinthians 7:1 speaks of '*having these promises,*' yet one of them, referred to in 6:18, is taken from the book of Leviticus!

Perhaps someone asks, 'But where am I to draw the line? Which of the Old Testament promises rightfully belong to me?' We answer that Psalm 84:11 declares, 'The Lord will give grace and glory: *no* good thing will He withhold from them that walk uprightly'. If you are really walking 'uprightly' you are entitled to appropriate that blessed promise and count upon the Lord giving you whatever 'good thing' is truly required by you. 'My God shall supply *all* your need' (Phil. 4:19). If then there is a promise anywhere in His Word which just fits your present case and situation, make it your own as suited to your 'need.' Steadfastly resist every attempt of Satan to rob you of any portion of your Father's Word.

4. We profit from the Word when *we make a proper discrimination between the promises of God*. Many of the Lord's people are frequently guilty of spiritual theft, by which we mean that they appropriate to themselves something to which they are not entitled, but which belongs to another. 'Certain covenant engagements, made with the Lord Jesus Christ, as to His elect and redeemed ones, are altogether without condition so far as we are concerned; but many other wealthy words of the Lord contain stipulations which must be carefully regarded, or we shall not obtain the blessing. One part of my reader's diligent search must be directed toward this most important point. God will keep His promise to thee; only see thou to it that the way in which He conditions His engagement is carefully observed by thee. Only when we fulfil the requirements of a conditional promise can we expect that promise to be fulfilled to us' (C. H. Spurgeon).

Many of the Divine promises are addressed to particular characters, or, more correctly speaking, to particular graces. For example, in Psalm 25:9, the Lord declares that He will 'guide in judgment' the *meek*; but if I am out of communion with Him, if I am following a course of self-will, if my heart is haughty, then I am not justified in taking to myself the comfort of this verse. Again, in John 15:7, the Lord tells us, 'If ye abide in me, and my words abide in you, ye shall ask what ye will, and it shall be done unto you.' But if I am not in experimental communion with Him, if His commands are not regulating my conduct, then my prayers will remain unanswered. While God's promises proceed from pure grace, yet it ever needs to be remembered that grace reigns 'through righteousness' (Rom. 5:21) and never sets aside human responsibility. If I ignore the laws of health I must not be surprised that sickness prevents me enjoying many of God's temporal mercies: in like manner, if I neglect His precepts I have myself to blame if I fail to receive the fulfilment of many of His promises.

Let none suppose that by His promises God has obligated Himself to ignore the requirements of His holiness: He never exercises any one of His perfections at the expense of another. And let none imagine that God would be magnifying the sacrificial work of Christ were He to bestow its fruits upon impenitent and careless souls. There is a *balance* of truth to be preserved here; alas, that it is now so frequently lost, and that under the pretence of exalting Divine grace men are really 'turning it into lasciviousness.' How often one hears quoted, 'Call upon me in the day of trouble: I will deliver thee' (Psa. 50:15). But that verse begins with 'And,' and the preceding clause is '*Pay thy vows* unto the most High!' Again, how frequently is 'I will guide thee with mine eye' (Psa. 32:8) seized by people who pay no attention to the context! But *that* is God's promise to one who has confessed his 'transgression' unto the Lord (verse 5). If, then, I have *un*confessed sin on my conscience, and have leaned on an arm of flesh or sought help from my fellows, instead of waiting only on God (Psa. 62:5), then I have no right to count upon the Lord's guiding me with His eye – which necessarily presupposes that I am walking in close communion with Him, for I cannot see the eye of another while at a distance from him.

5. We profit from the Word when *we are enabled to make God's promises our support and stay*. This is one reason why God has given them to us; not only to manifest His love by

making known His benevolent designs, but also to comfort our hearts and develop our faith. Had God so pleased He could have bestowed His blessings without giving us notice of His purpose. The Lord might have given us all the mercies we need without pledging Himself to do so. But in that case we could not have been believers; faith without a promise would be a foot without ground to stand upon. Our tender Father planned that we should enjoy His gifts twice over: first by faith, and then by fruition. By this means He wisely weans our hearts away from things seen and perishing and draws them onward and upward to those things which are spiritual and eternal.

If there were no promises there would not only be no faith, but no hope either. For what is hope but the *expectation* of the things which God has declared He will give us? Faith looks to the Word promising, hope looks to the performance thereof. Thus it was with Abraham; 'Who against hope believed in hope ... and being not weak in faith, he considered not his own body now dead, when he was about an hundred years old, neither yet the deadness of Sarah's womb; he staggered not ... through unbelief; but was strong in faith, giving glory to God' (Rom. 4:18, 20). Thus it was with Moses: 'Esteeming the reproach of Christ greater riches than the treasures in Egypt; for he had respect unto the recompense of the reward' (Heb. 11:26). Thus it was with Paul; 'I believe God, that it shall be even as it was told me' (Acts 27:25). Is it so with you, dear reader? Are the promises of Him who cannot lie the resting-place of your poor heart?

6. We profit from the Word when *we patiently await the fulfilment of God's promises*. God promised Abraham a son, but he waited many years for the performance of it. Simeon had a promise that he should not see death till he

had seen the Lord's Christ (Luke 2:26), yet it was not made good till he had one foot in the grave. There is often a long and hard winter between the sowing-time of prayer and the reaping of the answer. The Lord Jesus Himself has not yet received a full answer to the prayer He made in John chapter Seventeen, nineteen hundred years ago. Many of the best of God's promises to His people will not receive their richest accomplishment until they are in glory. He who has all eternity at His disposal needs not to hurry. God often makes us tarry so that patience may have 'her perfect work,' yet let us not distrust Him. 'For the vision is yet for an appointed time, but at the end it shall speak, and not lie: though it tarry, wait for it; because it will surely come' (Hab. 2:3).

'These all died in faith, not having received the [fulfilment of the] promises but having seen them afar off, and were persuaded of them, and embraced them' (Heb. 11: 13). Here is comprehended the whole work of faith: knowledge, trust, loving adherence. The 'afar off' refers to the things promised; those they 'saw' with the mind, discerning the substance behind the shadow, discovering in them the wisdom and goodness of God. They were 'persuaded': they doubted not, but were assured of their participation in them and knew they would not disappoint them. 'Embraced them' expresses their delight and veneration, the heart cleaving to them with love and cordially welcoming and entertaining them. The promises were the comfort and the stay of their souls in all their wanderings, temptations and sufferings.

Various ends are accomplished by God in delaying His execution of the promises. Not only is faith put to the proof, so that its genuineness may the more clearly appear; not only is patience developed, and hope given opportunity for exercise; but submission to the Divine will is fostered. 'The weaning process is not accomplished: we are still hankering after the comforts which the Lord intends us for ever to outgrow. Abraham made a great feast when his son Isaac was weaned; and, peradventure, our heavenly Father will do the same with us. Lie down, proud heart. Quit thine idols; forsake thy fond doings; and the promised peace will come unto thee' (C. H. Spurgeon).

7. We profit from the Word when *we make a right use of the promises*. First, in our dealings with God Himself. When we approach unto His throne, it should be to plead one of His promises. They are to form not only the foundation for our faith to rest upon, but also the substance of our requests. We must ask according to God's will if we are to be heard, and His will is revealed in those good things which He has declared He will bestow upon us. Thus we are to lay hold of His pledged assurances, spread them before Him, and say, 'Do as thou hast said' (2 Samuel 7:25). Observe how Jacob pleaded the promise in Genesis 32:12; Moses in Exodus 32:13; David in Psalm 119:58; Solomon in 1 Kings 8:25; and do thou, my Christian reader, likewise.

Second, in the life we live in the world. In Hebrews 11:13, we not only read of the patriarchs discerning, trusting, and embracing the Divine promises, but we are also informed of the *effects* which they produced upon them: 'and confessed that they were strangers and pilgrims in the earth,' which means they made a public avowal of their faith. They acknowledged (and by their conduct demonstrated) that their interests were not in the things of this world; they had a satisfying portion in the promises they had appropriated. Their hearts were set upon things above; for where a man's heart is, there will his treasure be also.

'Having therefore these promises, dearly beloved, let us cleanse ourselves from all filthiness of the flesh and spirit, perfecting holiness in the fear of God' (2 Cor. 7:1); that is the effect they should produce in us, and *will* if faith really lays hold of them. 'Whereby are given unto us exceeding great and precious promises: *that* by these ye might be partakers of the divine nature, having escaped the corruption that is in the world through lust' (2 Pet. 1:4). Now the Gospel and the precious promises, being graciously bestowed and powerfully applied, have an influence on purity of heart and behaviour, and teach men to deny ungodliness and worldly lusts, and to live soberly, righteously, and godly. Such are the powerful effects of gospel promises under the Divine influence as to make men inwardly partakers of the Divine nature and outwardly to abstain from and avoid the prevailing corruptions and vices of the times.

9: *The Scriptures and Joy*

THE ungodly are ever seeking after joy, but they do not find it: they busy and weary themselves in the pursuit of it, yet all in vain. Their hearts being turned from the Lord, they look downward for joy, where it is not; rejecting the substance, they diligently run after the shadow, only to be mocked by it. It is the sovereign decree of heaven that nothing can make sinners truly happy but God in Christ; but this they will not believe, and therefore they go from creature to creature, from one broken cistern to another, inquiring where the best joy is to be found. Each worldly thing which attracts them says, It is found in me; but soon it disappoints. Nevertheless, they go on seeking it afresh today in the very thing which deceived them yesterday. If after many trials they discover the emptiness of one creature comfort, then they turn to another, only to verify our Lord's word, 'Whosoever drinketh of this water shall thirst again' (John 4:13).

Going now to the other extreme: there are some Christians who suppose it to be sinful to rejoice. No doubt many of our readers will be surprised to hear this but let them be thankful they have been brought up in sunnier surroundings, and bear with us while we labour with those less favoured. Some have been taught – largely by implication and example, rather than by plain inculcation – that it is their duty to be gloomy. They imagine that feelings of joy are produced by the Devil appearing as an angel of light. They conclude that it is well-nigh a species of wickedness to be happy in such a world of sin as we are in. They think it presumptuous to rejoice in the knowledge of sins forgiven, and if they see young Christians so doing they tell them it will not be long before they are floundering in the Slough of Despond. To all such we tenderly urge the prayerful pondering of the remainder of this chapter.

'Rejoice evermore' (1 Thess. 5:16). It surely cannot be unsafe to do what God has commanded us. The Lord has placed no embargo on rejoicing. No, it is Satan who strives to make us hang up our harps. There is no precept in Scripture bidding us 'Grieve in the Lord alway: and again I say, Grieve'; but there is an exhortation which bids us, 'Rejoice in the Lord, O ye righteous: for praise is comely for the upright' (Psa. 33:1). Reader, if you are a real Christian (and it is high time you tested yourself by Scripture and made sure of this point), then Christ is yours, all that is in Him is yours. He bids you 'Eat, O friends; drink, yea, drink *abundantly*, O beloved' (Song of Sol. 5:1): the only sin you may commit against His banquet of love is to stint yourself. 'Let your soul delight itself *in fatness*'(Isa. 55:2) is spoken not to those already in heaven but to saints still on earth. This leads us to say that:

1. We profit from the Word when we perceive that *joy is a duty*. 'Rejoice in the Lord alway: and again I say, Rejoice' (Phil. 4:4). The Holy Spirit here speaks of rejoicing as a personal, present and permanent duty for the people of God to carry out. The Lord has not left it to our option whether we should be glad or sad, but has made happiness an obligation. Not to rejoice is a sin of omission. Next time you meet with a radiant Christian, do not chide him, ye dwellers in Doubting Castle, but chide yourselves; instead

of being ready to call into question the Divine spring of his mirth, judge yourself for your doleful state.

It is not a carnal joy which we are here urging, by which we mean a joy which comes from carnal sources. It is useless to seek joy in earthly riches, for frequently they take to themselves wings and fly away. Some seek their joy in the family circle, but that remains entire for only a few years at most. No, if we are to 'rejoice evermore' it must be in an object that lasts for evermore. Nor is it a fanatical joy we have reference to. There are some with an excitable nature who are happy only when they are half out of their minds; but terrible is the reaction. No, it is an intelligent, steady, heart delight in God Himself. Every attribute of God, when contemplated by faith, will make the heart sing. Every doctrine of the Gospel, when truly apprehended, will call forth gladness and praise.

Joy is a matter of Christian duty. Perhaps the reader is ready to exclaim, My emotions of joy and sorrow are not under my control; I cannot help being glad or sad as circumstances dictate. But we repeat, 'Rejoice in the Lord' is a Divine command, and to a large extent obedience to it lies in one's own power. I am responsible to control my emotions. True, I cannot help being sorrowful in the presence of sorrowful thoughts, but I can refuse to let my mind dwell upon them. I can pour out my heart for relief unto the Lord, and cast my burden upon Him. I can seek grace to meditate upon His goodness, His promises, the glorious future awaiting me. I have to decide whether I will go and stand in the light or hide among the shadows. Not to rejoice in the Lord is more than a misfortune, it is a fault which needs to be confessed and forsaken.

2. We profit from the Word when *we learn the secret of true joy*. That secret is revealed in 1 John 1:3, 4: 'Truly

our fellowship is with the Father, and with his Son Jesus Christ. And these things write we unto you, that your joy may be full.' When we consider the littleness of our fellowship with God, the shallowness of it, it is not to be wondered at that so many Christians are comparatively joyless. We sometimes sing, 'Oh happy day that fixed my choice on Thee, my Saviour and my God! Well may this glowing heart rejoice and tell its raptures all abroad.' Yes, but if that happiness is to be maintained there must be a continued steadfast occupation of the heart and mind with Christ. It is only where there is much faith and consequent love that there is much joy.

'Rejoice *in the Lord* alway.' There is no other object in which we can rejoice 'alway.' Everything else varies and is inconstant. What pleases us today may pall on us tomorrow. But the Lord is always the same, to be enjoyed in seasons of adversity as much as in seasons of prosperity. As an aid to this, the very next verse says, 'Let your *moderation* be known unto all men. The Lord is at hand' (Phil. 4:5). Be temperate in connection with all external things; do not be taken with them when they seem most pleasing, nor troubled when displeasing. Be not exalted when the world smiles upon you, nor dejected when it scowls. Maintain a stoical indifference to outward comforts: why be so occupied with them when *the Lord Himself* 'is at hand'? If persecution be violent, if temporal losses be heavy, the Lord is 'a very *present help* in trouble' (Psa. 46:1) – ready to support and succour those who cast themselves upon Him. He will care for you, so 'be anxious for nothing' (Phil. 4:6). Worldlings are haunted with carking cares, but the Christian should not be.

'These things have I spoken unto you, that my joy might remain in you, and that your joy might be full'

(John 15:11). As these precious words of Christ are pondered by the mind and treasured in the heart, they cannot but produce joy. A rejoicing heart comes from an increasing knowledge of and love for the truth as it is in Jesus. 'Thy words were found, and I did eat them; and thy word was unto me the joy and rejoicing of mine heart' (Jer. 15:16). Yes, it is by feeding and feasting upon the words of the Lord that the soul is made fat, and we are made to sing and make melody in our hearts unto Him.

'Then will I go unto the altar of God, unto God my exceeding joy' (Psa. 43:4). As Spurgeon well said, 'With what exultation should believers draw near unto Christ, who is the antitype of the altar! Clearer light should give greater intensity of desire. It was not the altar as such that the Psalmist cared for, for he was no believer in the heathenism of ritualism: his soul desired spiritual fellowship, fellowship with God Himself in very deed. What are all the rites of worship unless the Lord be in them; what, indeed, but empty shells and dry husks? Note the holy rapture with which David regards his Lord! He is not his joy alone, but his *exceeding* joy; not the fountain of joy, the giver of joy, or the maintainer of joy, but *that joy itself*. The margin hath it, "The gladness of my joy"; i.e. the soul, the essence, the very bowels of my joy.'

'Although the fig tree shall not blossom, neither shall fruit be in the vines; the labour of the olive shall fail, and the fields shall yield no meat; the flock shall be cut off from the fold, and there shall be no herd in the stalls: yet I will rejoice in *the Lord*, I will joy in the God of my salvation' (Hab. 3:17, 18). That is something of which the worldling knows nothing; alas, that it is an experience to which so many professing Christians are strangers! It is in God that the fount of spiritual and everlasting joy originates;

from Him it all flows forth. This was acknowledged of old by the Church when she said, 'All my springs are in thee' (Psa. 87:7). Happy the soul who has been truly taught this secret!

3. We profit from the Word when we are taught *the great value of joy*. Joy is to the soul what wings are to the bird, enabling us to soar above the things of earth. This is brought out plainly in Nehemiah 8:10: 'The joy of the Lord is *your strength*.' The days of Nehemiah marked a turning-point in the history of Israel. A remnant had been freed from Babylon and returned to Palestine. The Law, long ignored by the captives, was now to be established again as the rule of the newly-formed commonwealth. There had come a remembrance of the many sins of the past, and tears not unnaturally mingled with the thankfulness that they were again a nation, having a Divine worship and a Divine Law in their midst. Their leader, knowing full well that if the spirit of the people began to flag they could not face and conquer the difficulties of their position, said to them: 'This day is holy unto the Lord: (this feast we are keeping is a day of devout worship; therefore, mourn not), neither be ye sorry, for the joy of the Lord is your strength.'

Confession of sin and mourning over the same have their place, and communion with God cannot be maintained without them. Nevertheless, when true repentance has been exercised, and things put right with God, we must forget 'those things which are behind' and reach forth unto 'those things which are before' (Phil. 3:13). And we can only press forward with alacrity as our hearts are joyful. How heavy the steps of him who approaches the place where a loved one lies cold in death! How energetic his movements as he goes forth to meet his bride! Lamentation unfits for the battles of life. Where there is despair there is no longer power for obedience. If there be no joy, there can be no worship.

My dear readers, there are tasks needing to be performed, service to others requiring to be rendered, temptations to be overcome, battles to be fought; and we are only experimentally fitted for them as our hearts are rejoicing in the Lord. If our souls are resting in Christ, if our hearts are filled with a tranquil gladness, work will be easy, duties pleasant, sorrow bearable, endurance possible. Neither contrite remembrance of past failures nor vehement resolutions will carry us through. If the arm is to smite with vigour, it must smite at the bidding of a light heart. Of the Saviour Himself it is recorded, 'Who for the *joy that was set before him* endured the cross, despising the shame' (Heb. 12:2).

4. We profit from the Word when we attend to *the root of joy*. The spring of joy is faith: 'Now the God of hope fill you with all peace and joy in believing' (Rom. 15:13). There is a wondrous provision in the Gospel, both by what it takes from us and what it brings to us, to give a calm and settled glow to the Christian's heart. It takes away the load of guilt by speaking peace to the stricken conscience. It removes the dread of God and the terror of death which weighs on the soul while it is under condemnation. It gives us God Himself as the portion of our hearts, as the object of our communion. The Gospel works joy, because the soul is at rest in God. But these blessings become our own only by personal appropriation. Faith must *receive* them, and when it does so the heart is filled with peace and joy. And the secret of *sustained* joy is to keep the channel open, to continue as we began. It is *unbelief* which clogs the channel. If there be but little heat around the bulb of the

thermometer, no wonder that the mercury marks so low a degree. If there is a weak faith, joy cannot be strong. Daily do we need to pray for a *fresh* realization of the preciousness of the Gospel, a fresh appropriation of its blessed contents; and then there will be a renewing of our joy.

5. We profit from the Word when *we are careful to maintain our joy*. 'Joy in the Holy Spirit' is altogether different from a natural buoyancy of spirit. It is the product of the Comforter dwelling in our hearts and bodies, revealing Christ to us, answering all our need for pardon and cleansing, and so setting us at peace with God; and forming Christ in us, so that He reigns in our souls, subduing us to His control. There are no circumstances of trial and temptation in which we may refrain from it, for the command is, 'Rejoice in the Lord *alway*.' He who gave this command knows all about the dark side of our lives, the sins and sorrows which beset us, the 'much tribulation' through which we must enter the kingdom of God. Natural hilarity leaves the woes of our earthly lot out of its reckoning. It soon relaxes in the presence of life's hardships: it cannot survive the loss of friends or health. But the joy to which we are exhorted is not limited to any set of circumstances or type of temperament; nor does it fluctuate with our varying moods and fortunes.

Nature may assert itself in the subjects of it, as even Jesus wept at the grave of Lazarus. Nevertheless, they can exclaim with Paul, 'As sorrowful, yet alway rejoicing' (2 Cor. 6:10). The Christian may be loaded with heavy responsibilities, his life may have a series of reverses, his plans may be thwarted and his hopes blighted, the grave may close over the loved ones who gave his earthly life its cheer and sweetness, and yet, under all his disappointments and sorrows, his Lord still bids him 'Rejoice.' Behold the apostles in Philippi's prison, in the innermost dungeon, with feet fast in the stocks, and backs bleeding and smarting from the terrible scourging they had received. How were they occupied? In grumbling and growling? in asking what they had done to deserve such treatment? No! At midnight Paul and Silas prayed and *sang* praises unto God' (Acts 16:25). There was no sin in their lives, they were walking obediently, and so the Holy Spirit was free to take of the things of Christ, and show them unto their hearts, so that they were filled to overflowing. If we are to maintain our joy, we must keep from grieving the Holy Spirit.

When Christ is supreme in the heart, joy fills it. When He is Lord of every desire, the Source of every motive, the Subjugator of every lust, then will joy fill the heart and praise ascend from the lips. The possession of this involves taking up the cross every hour of the day; God has so ordered it that we cannot have the one without the other. Self-sacrifice, the cutting off of a right hand, the plucking out of a right eye, are the avenues through which the Spirit enters the soul, bringing with Him the joys of God's approving smile and the assurance of His love and abiding presence. Much also depends upon the spirit in which we enter the world each day. If we expect people to pet and pamper us, disappointment will make us fretful. If we desire our pride to be ministered to, we are dejected when it is not. The secret of happiness is forgetting self and seeking to minister to the happiness of others. 'It is more blessed to give than to receive,' so it is a happier thing to minister to others than to be ministered to.

6. We profit from the Word when *we are sedulous in avoiding the hindrances to joy*. Why is it that so many

Christians have so little joy? Are they not all born children of the light and of the day? This term 'light,' which is so often used in Scripture to describe to us the nature of God, our relations to Him and our future destiny, is most suggestive of joy and gladness. What other thing in nature is as beneficent and beautiful as the light? 'God is light, and in Him is no darkness at all (1 John 1:5). It is only as we walk with God, in the light, that the heart can truly be joyous. It is the deliberate allowing of things which mar our fellowship with Him that chills and darkens our souls. It is the indulgence of the flesh, the fraternizing with the world, the entering of forbidden paths which blight our spiritual lives and make us cheerless.

David had to cry, 'Restore unto me *the joy of* thy salvation' (Psa. 51:12). He had grown lax and self-indulgent. Temptation presented itself and he had no power to resist. He yielded, and one sin led to another. He was a backslider, out of touch with God. Unconfessed sin lay heavy on his conscience. Oh my brethren and sisters, if we are to be kept from such a fall, if we are not to lose our joy, then self must be denied, the affections and lusts of the flesh crucified. We must ever be on our watch against temptation. We must spend much time upon our knees. We must drink frequently from the Fountain of living waters. We must be out-and-out for the Lord.

7. We profit from the Word when *we diligently preserve the balance between sorrow and joy*. If the Christian faith has a marked adaptation to produce joy, it has an almost equal design and tendency to produce sorrow – a sorrow that is solemn, manly, noble. 'As sorrowful, yet always rejoicing' (2 Cor. 6:10) is the rule of the Christian's life. If faith casts its light upon our condition, our nature, our sins, sadness must be one of the effects. There is nothing

more contemptible in itself, and there is no surer mark of a superficial character and trivial round of occupation, than unshaded gladness, that rests on no deep foundations of quiet, patient grief – grief because I know what I am and what I ought to be; grief because I look out on the world and see hell's fire burning at the back of mirth and laughter, and know *what* it is that men are hurrying to.

He who is anointed with the oil of gladness above His fellows (Psa. 45:7) was also 'the man *of sorrows* and acquainted with *grief*.' And both of these characters are (in measure) repeated in the operations of His Gospel upon every heart that really receives it. And if, on the one hand, by the fears it removes from us and the hopes it breathes into us, and the fellowship into which it introduces us, we are anointed with the oil of gladness; on the other hand, by the sense of our own vileness which it teaches us, by the conflict between the flesh and the Spirit, there is infused a sadness which finds expression in 'O wretched man that I am!' (Rom. 7:24). These two are not contradictory but complementary. The Lamb must be eaten with 'bitter herbs' (Ex. 12:8).

10: *The Scriptures and Love*

IN earlier chapters we have sought to point out some of the ways by which we may ascertain whether or not our reading and searching of the Scriptures are really being blessed to our souls. Many are deceived on this matter, mistaking an eagerness to acquire knowledge for a spiritual love of the Truth (2 Thess. 2:10), and assuming that addition to their store of learning is the same thing as growth in grace. A great deal depends upon the end or aim we have before us when turning to God's Word. If it be simply to familiarize ourselves with its contents and become better versed in its details, it is likely that the garden of our souls will remain barren; but if with the prayerful desire to be rebuked and corrected by the Word, to be searched by the Spirit, to conform our hearts to its holy requirements, then we may expect a Divine blessing.

In the preceding chapters we have endeavoured to single out the vital things by which we may discover what progress we are making in personal godliness. Various criteria have been given, which it becomes both writer and reader honestly to measure themselves by. We have pressed such tests as: Am I acquiring a greater hatred of sin, and a practical deliverance from its power and pollution? Am I obtaining a deeper acquaintance with God and His Christ? Is my prayer-life healthier? Are my good works more abundant? Is my obedience fuller and gladder? Am I more separated from the world in my affections and ways? Am I learning to make a right and profitable use of God's promises, and so delighting myself in Him that His joy is my daily strength? Unless I can truthfully say that these are (in some measure) my experience, then it is greatly to be feared that my study of the Scriptures is profiting me little or nothing.

It hardly seems fitting that these chapters should be concluded until one has been devoted to the consideration of Christian love. The extent to which this spiritual grace is, or is not, being cultivated and regulated affords another index to the measure in which my perusal of God's Word is helping me spiritually. No one can read the Scriptures with any measure of attention without discovering how much they have to say about love, and therefore it behoves each one of us prayerfully and carefully to ascertain whether or not his or her love be really a spiritual one, and whether it be in a healthy state and is being exercised aright.

The subject of Christian love is far too comprehensive to consider all its varied phases within the compass of a single chapter. Properly we should begin with contemplating the exercise of our love toward God and His Christ, but as this has been at least touched upon in preceding chapters we shall now waive it. Much too, might be said about the natural love which we owe to our fellow-men, who belong to the same family as we do, but there is less need to write on that theme than on what is now before our mind. Here we propose to confine our attention to spiritual love to the brethren, the brethren of Christ.

1. We profit from the Word when *we perceive the great importance of Christian love*. Nowhere is this brought out more emphatically than in 1 Corinthians chapter 13.

There the Holy Spirit tells us that though a professing Christian can speak fluently and eloquently upon Divine things, if has not love, he is like metal, which, though it makes a noise when struck, is lifeless. That though he can prophesy, understand all mysteries and knowledge, and has faith which brings miracles to pass, yet if he be lacking in love, he is spiritually a nonentity. Yea, that though he be so benevolent as to give all his worldly possessions to feed the poor, and yield his body to a martyr's death, yet if he have not love, it profits him nothing. How high a value is here placed upon love, and how essential for me to make sure I possess it!

Said our Lord, 'By this shall all men know that ye are my disciples, if ye have love one to another' (John 13:35). By Christ's making it the badge of Christian discipleship, we see again the great importance of love. It is an essential test of the genuineness of our profession: we cannot love Christ unless we love His brethren, for they are all bound up in the same 'bundle of life' (1 Samuel 25:29) with Him. Love to those whom He has redeemed is a sure evidence of spiritual and supernatural love to the Lord Jesus Himself. Where the Holy Spirit has wrought a supernatural birth, He will draw forth that nature into exercise, He will produce in the hearts and lives and conduct of the saints supernatural graces, one of which is loving all who are Christ's for Christ's sake.

2. We profit from the Word when *we learn to detect the sad perversions of Christian love*. As water will not rise above its own level, so the natural man is incapable of understanding, still less appreciating, that which is spiritual (1 Cor. 2:14). Therefore we should not be surprised when unregenerate professors mistake human sentimentality and carnal pleasantries for spiritual love. But sad it is to

see some of God's own people living on so low a plane that they confuse human amiability and affability with the queen of the Christian graces. While it is true that spiritual love is characterized by meekness and gentleness, yet is it something very different from and vastly superior to the courtesies and kindnesses of the flesh.

How many a doting father has withheld the rod from his children, under the mistaken notion that real affection for them and the chastising of them were incompatible! How many a foolish mother, who disdained all corporal punishment, has boasted that 'love' rules in her home! One of the most trying experiences of the writer, in his extensive travels, has been to spend a season in homes where the children have been completely spoilt. It is a wicked perversion of the word 'love' to apply it to moral laxity and parental looseness. But this same pernicious idea rules the minds of many people in other connections and relations. If a servant of God rebukes their fleshly and worldly ways, if he presses the uncompromising claims of God, he is at once charged with being 'lacking in love.' Oh, how terribly are multitudes deceived by Satan on this important subject!

3. We profit from the Word when we are taught the *true nature of Christian love*. Christian love is a spiritual grace abiding in the souls of the saints alongside faith and hope (I Cor. 13:13). It is a holy disposition wrought in them when they are regenerated (1 John 5:1). It is nothing less than the love of God shed abroad in their hearts by the Holy Spirit (Rom. 5:5). It is a righteous principle which seeks the highest good of others. It is the very reverse of that principle of self-love and self-seeking which is in us by nature. It is not only an affectionate regard of all who bear the image of Christ, but also a powerful desire to pro-

mote their welfare. It is not a fickle sentiment which is easily offended, but an abiding dynamic which 'many waters' of cold indifference or 'floods' of disapproval can neither quench nor drown (Song of Sol. 8:7). Though coming far short in degree it is the same in essence as His of whom we read, 'Having loved his own which were in the world, he loved them unto the end' (John 13:1).

There is no safer and surer way of obtaining a right conception of the nature of Christian love than by making a thorough study of its perfect exemplification in and by the Lord Jesus. When we say a 'thorough study,' we mean the taking of a comprehensive survey of *all* that is recorded of Him in the four Gospels, and not the limiting of ourselves to a few favourite passages or incidents. As this is done, we discover that His love was not only benevolent and magnanimous, thoughtful and gentle, unselfish and self-sacrificing, patient and unchanging, but that many other elements also entered into it. Love could deny an urgent request (John 11:6), rebuke His mother (John 2:4), use a whip (John 2:15), severely upbraid His doubting disciples (Luke 24:25), and denounce hypocrites (Matt. 23:13–33). Love can be stern (Matt. 16:23), yea, angry (Mark 3:5). Spiritual love is a *holy* thing: it is faithful to God; it is uncompromising toward all that is evil.

4. We profit from the Word when *we discover that Christian love is a Divine communication*. 'We know that we have passed from death unto life, because we love the brethren' (1 John 3:14). 'Love to the brethren is the fruit and effect of a new and supernatural birth, wrought in our souls by the Holy Spirit, as the blessed evidence of our having been chosen in Christ by the Divine Father, before the world was. To love Christ and His, and our brethren in Him, is congenial to that Divine nature He hath made us

119

the partakers of by His Holy Spirit. . . . This love of the brethren must be a peculiar love, such as none but the regenerate are the subjects of, and which none but they can exercise, or the apostle would not have so particularly mentioned it; it is such that those who have it not are in a state of unregeneracy; so it follows, "he that loveth not his brother abideth in death" ' (S. E. Pierce).

Love for the brethren is far, far more than finding agreeable the society of those whose temperaments are similar to or whose views accord with my own. It pertains not to mere nature, but is a spiritual and supernatural thing. It is the heart being drawn out to those in whom I perceive *something of Christ*. Thus it is very much more than a party spirit; it embraces all in whom I can see the image of God's Son. It is, therefore, a loving them for Christ's sake, for what I see of Christ in them. It is the Holy Spirit within attracting and alluring me with Christ indwelling my brethren and sisters. Thus real Christian love is not only a Divine gift, but is altogether dependent upon God for its invigoration and exercise. We need to pray daily that the Holy Spirit will call forth into action and manifestation, toward both God and His people, that love which He has shed abroad in our hearts.

5. We profit from the Word when *we rightly exercise Christian love*. This is done, not by seeking to please our brethren and ingratiate ourselves in their esteem, but when we truly seek their highest good. 'By this we know that we love the children of God, when we love God, and keep his commandments' (1 John 5:2). What is the real test of my personal love to God Himself? It is my keeping of His commandments (see John 14:15, 21, 24; 15:10, 14). The genuineness and strength of my love to God are not to be measured by my words, nor by the lustiness with

which I sing His praises, but by my obedience to His Word. The same principle holds good in my relations with my brethren.

'By this we know that we love the children of God, when we love God, and keep His commandments.' If I am glossing over the faults of my brethren and sisters, if I am walking with them in a course of self-will and self-pleasing, then I am *not* 'loving' them. 'Thou shalt not hate thy brother in thine heart: thou shalt in any wise rebuke thy neighbour, and not suffer sin upon him' (Lev. 19:17). Love is to be exercised in a Divine way, and never at the expense of my failing to love God; in fact, it is only when God has His proper place in my heart that spiritual love can be exercised by me toward my brethren. True spiritual love does not consist in gratifying them, but in pleasing God and helping them; and I can only *help* them in the path of God's commandments.

Petting and pampering one another is not brotherly love; exhorting one another to press forward in the race that is set before us, and speaking words (enforced by the example of our daily walk) which will encourage them to 'look off unto Jesus,' would be much more helpful. Brotherly love is a holy thing, and not a fleshly sentiment or a loose indifference as to the path we are treading. God's 'commandments' are expressions of His love, as well as of His authority, and to ignore them, even while seeking to be kindly affectioned one to another, is not 'love' at all. The *exercise* of love is to be in strict conformity to the revealed will of God. We are to love 'in the truth' (3 John 1).

6. We profit from the Word when *we are taught the varied manifestations of Christian love*. To love our brethren and manifest the love in all kinds of ways is our

bounden duty. But at no point can we do this more truly and effectually, and with less affectation and ostentation, than by having fellowship with them at the throne of grace. There are brethren and sisters in Christ in the four corners of the earth, about the details of whose trials and conflicts, temptations and sorrows, I know nothing; yet I can express my love for them, and pour out my heart before God on their behalf, by earnest supplication and intercession. In no other way can the Christian more manifest his affectionate regard toward his fellow-pilgrims than by using all his interests in the Lord Jesus in their behalf, intreating His mercies and favours unto them.

'Whoso hath this world's good, and seeth his brother have need, and shutteth up his bowels of compassion from him, how dwelleth the love of God in him? My little children, let us not love in word, neither in tongue; but in deed and in truth' (1 John 3:17, 18). Many of God's people are very poor in this world's goods. Sometimes they wonder why it is so; it is a great trial to them. One reason why the Lord permits this is that others of His saints may have their compassion drawn out and minister to their temporal needs from the abundance with which God has furnished them. Real love is intensely practical: it considers no office too mean, no task too humbling, where the sufferings of a brother can be relieved. When the Lord of love was here upon earth, He had thought for the bodily hunger of the multitude and the comfort of His disciples' feet!

But there are some of the Lord's people so poor that they have very little indeed to share with others. What, then, may they do? Why, make the spiritual concerns of all the saints their own; interest themselves on their behalf at the throne of grace! We know by our own cases and circumstances what the feelings, sorrows, and complaints of other saints must be the subjects of. We know from sad experience how easy it is to give way to a spirit of discontent and murmuring. But we also know how, when we have cried unto the Lord for His quieting hand to be laid upon us, and when He has brought some precious promise to our remembrance, what peace and comfort have come to our heart. Then let us beg Him to be equally gracious to all His distressed saints. Let us seek to make their burdens our own, and weep with them that weep, as well as rejoice with them that rejoice. Thus shall we express real love for their persons in Christ by intreating their Lord and our Lord to remember them with everlasting kindness.

This is how the Lord Jesus is now manifesting *His* love to His saints: 'He ever liveth to make intercession for them' (Heb. 7:25). He makes their cause and care His own. He is intreating the Father on their behalf. None is forgotten by Him: every lone sheep is borne upon the heart of the Good Shepherd. Thus, by expressing our love to the brethren in daily prayers for the supply of their varied needs, we are brought into fellowship with our great High Priest. Not only so, but the saints will be endeared to us thereby: our very praying for them as the beloved of God will increase our love and esteem for them as such. We cannot carry them on our hearts before the throne of grace without cherishing in our own hearts a real affection for them. The best way of overcoming a bitter spirit to a brother who has offended is to be much in prayer for him.

7. We profit from the Word when *we are taught the proper cultivation of Christian love*. We suggest two or three rules for this. First, recognizing at the outset that just as there is much in you (in me) which will severely try the love of the brethren, so there will be not a little in

them to test our love. '*Forbearing* one another in love'
(Eph. 4:3) is a great admonition on this subject which each
of us needs to lay to heart. It is surely striking to note that
the very first quality of spiritual love named in 1 Corinthians 13 is that it '*suffereth* long' (verse 4).

Second, the best way to cultivate any virtue or grace is
to *exercise* it. Talking and theorizing about it avails nothing unless it be carried into action. Many are the complaints heard today about the littleness of the love which is
being manifested in many places: that is all the more reason why I should seek to set a better example! Suffer not
the coldness and unkindliness of others to dampen your
love, but 'overcome evil with good' (Romans. 12:21).
Prayerfully ponder 1 Corinthians 13 at least once a week.

Third, above all, see to it that your own heart basks in
the light and warmth of God's love. Like begets like. The
more you are truly occupied with the unwearying, unfail-
ing, unfathomable love of Christ to you, the more will your
heart be drawn out in love to those who are His. A beautiful illustration of this is found in the fact that the particular apostle who wrote most upon brotherly love was he
who leaned upon the Master's bosom. The Lord grant all
requisite grace to both reader and writer (than whom none
more needs to heed them) to observe these rules, to the
praise of the glory of His grace, and to the good of His
beloved people.

SOME OTHER
BANNER OF TRUTH TRUST
TITLES

THE SOVEREIGNTY OF GOD *
A. W. Pink

At a time when there is renewed discussion on this contro-
versial subject, this popular reprint of A. W. Pink's well-
known work provides a clear and forthright statement of
Divine sovereignty in creation, providence and redemption.
But the author does more than expound the Scriptural doctrine. At every point he applies this truth to present-day
conditions and shows its relevance to much contemporary
teaching.

'Present day conditions', writes the author, 'call loudly
for a new examination and new presentation of God's
omnipotence, God's sufficiency, God's sovereignty. From
every pulpit in the land it needs to be thundered forth that
God still lives, that God still observes, that God still reigns.
Faith is now in the crucible, it is being tested by fire, and
there is no fixed and sufficient resting-place for the heart
and mind but in the Throne of God. What is needed now,
as never before, is a full, positive, constructive setting forth
of the Godhood of God.'

Paperback, 160 *pages*, 30p

THE LIFE OF ELIJAH
A. W. Pink

The life of Elijah has gripped the thought and imagination of preachers and writers in all ages. His sudden appearance out of complete obscurity, his dramatic interventions in the national history of Israel, his miracles, his departure from earth in a chariot of fire all serve to that end. 'He comes in like a tempest, who went out like a whirlwind', says Bishop Hall; 'the first that we hear from him is an oath and a threat'. Judgment and mercy were mingled throughout Elijah's astonishing career.

It is fitting that the lessons which may be drawn from Elijah's ministry should be presented afresh to our generation. History repeats itself. The wickedness and idolatry rampant in Ahab's reign live on in our gross 20th century's profanities and corruptions. False prophets occupy large spheres of influence and truths dear to our evangelical forefathers have been down trodden as the mire of the streets. A. W. Pink clearly felt called to the task of smiting the ungodliness of the age with the rod of God's anger while at the same time encouraging the faithful remnant. With these objects he undertakes the exposition of Elijah's ministry and applies it to the contemporary situation.

Paperback, 320 pages, 40p

Some Other Paperback Titles